Fighting Men of Texas

Fighting Men of Texas

Texas history tales
in blank verse

Mary Lou Burkett

EAKIN PRESS
Austin, Texas

Library of Congress Cataloging-in-Publication Data

Burkett, Mary Lou, 1909–
    Fighting men of Texas.

    1. Texas — History, Military — Poetry.   2. War poetry, American.   I. Title.
PS3552.U7244F5   811'.54   86-16594
ISBN 0-89015-571-2

FIRST EDITION

Copyright © 1986
By Mary Lou Burkett

Published in the United States of America
By Eakin Press, P.O. Box 23066, Austin, Texas 78735

ISBN 0-89015-571-2

Illustrations by Joan Hilbig

Contents

Preface

Although it may be a generally accepted fact that a poet does not list references, this author is deeply indebted to those who have studied, analyzed, and preserved records of the Texas past.

Letters of Travis, Houston, Green, and others have been quoted. Just as written, the expressions of these men are poetic. They fit beautifully into the pattern of the poem. With few exceptions, the words are as originally written. Only the form has been changed.

Fighting Men of Texas

I sing of fighting men who loved their land
When hostile peoples of another tongue,
When enemies who lived by other laws,
When those who sought to force them into one,
And only one great church, excluding all
The freedom of a man to make his choice, —
When all but Heaven seemed against their lot
And would have forced them from their prairie homes!

I sing of fighting men who loved their land:
Of men who stayed and fought, and so became
The first to know and earn the mighty name,
The term that rang above a thundering herd
Of buffalo, or lifted valor high
Above a bloody Indian massacre.
Who then could say, or who will ever name
A greater honor to those men who fought,
(Those men who loved the tidelands and the hills
Of yet so vast a land, a hallowed place)
Than just the plain and mighty name of *Texan?*

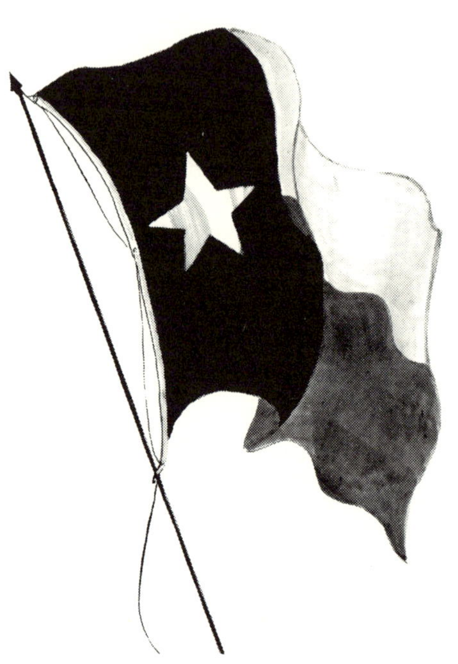

The Naming of Texas

Fourteen score and sixteen years ago
When Indian tribes roamed Texas' piney woods,
A Spanish priest, named Father Massanet,
Extended them a Christian hand in faith
To give them knowledge of the world and God.

The Hasinai confederacy was large,
And of the tribes, the Tejas Indian stood
The friendliest — the native of the forest
Whose home was found among the scented pines —
Thus Father Massanet attributed
A goodness to the land, and from the Tejas
Came the strong and friendly name of Texas.

How strange, and how miraculous this place
Wherein so many climes and cultures thrive —
Deep seaports, Magic Valley, hills, and sand!
The Coastal Plains and Coastal Prairie stretch
For miles. The Piney Woods, the Post-Oak Belt,
Redlands of the east, and Cap Rock, west,
The rivers and the lakes, from Red to Rio Grande, —
The timberlands, the plains, the plateau wide!
Vast wealth beyond our understanding lies
In fertile fields; rich minerals range below.

The seeds of many nations burst the soil;
The horses, cattle, wild game, fish, and birds
Indicative of influxes of breeds
From several lands across the mighty seas
Prove once and over — many, many times
The infiltration of the ages past
When Spanish, French, and then a melting pot
Of other cultures came to add their weight,
While Redmen and bold pirates fought to live
And plant their names and color in the land.

Flashes into the Past

From Europe, men from Spain were first to come,
Exploring Texas shores and timberlands,
Discovering the canyons and the plains;
And, bringing cattle, they began the growth
Of Texas cattle herds we have today.
They named the Palo Duro and the bays —
And many rivers, too, took on their names —
But, most of all, they searched the land for gold
And silver, which they seldom found at all —
And yet their imprint lingers in the land.

Columbus' voyage in 1492
Opened the gateway to America:
First, Santo Domingo and the West Indies,
And Mexico with metals and fine stones;
While Texas, then, seemed only barren land,
Cortez was leading men in Mexico;
Pineda sailed the Gulf of Mexico
In sight of Texas when he sought a strait
To lead, he hoped, to an East Indies route,
So long the purpose of the men who sailed
And dreamed of trade and riches in the world.

In 1528, Cabeza de Vaca
And some survivors of the company
Narvaez took to Florida were cast
Upon an island shore called Malhado,
Now known as Galveston. Ill fortune reigned,
And tribes of Indians were kind or hard
By turns. He always strove to find a way
To Spanish settlements, and so he roamed
To Matagorda Bay, and then northwest.
He followed close the Colorado's course
To San Saba, then west to the Pecos River,

On to the Rio Grande, El Paso then —
He finally returned to Spain to tell
His Texas wanderings of many years;
And so, De Vaca is remembered long
Because he was the first white man to cross
The territory of an untried land.

De Soto's expedition, next for Spain,
Touched Florida and all the great Southeast;
Upon De Soto's death, Moscoso led
The remnants of this expedition west.
They crossed the Red River and the timberlands
Before their explorations led them back
To the Mississippi and to Mexico, —
And thus, they had explored East Texas lands
Upon this expedition Europe sent.

Francisco Coronado, next for Spain,
Came through the western part, on leading men
To find the Seven Cities of Cibola.
Fruitless as the search became, they learned
Some things of northwest Texas and the tribes
Of Indians, and of their hunts for buffalo, —
But Spain was not impressed with such a land.

And when the sixteenth century was late,
Remaining just a score of years, the mines
In Durango and Zacatecas glowed.
Slave hunters crossed the Rio Grande for men
And captured Indians to work the mines.
Franciscan friars followed after them,
And missionary work brought early bloom.

And, as the century closed, the Spaniards knew
The land, not so much for itself, as for
A way between New Mexico and Old —
There was a cattle trail through El Paso,
A long and dusty trail — no settlers stayed.
But missions grew along the Rio Grande

As Spanish parties entered later on
Along that part that bounds the present state.
In 1659 Juarez was born,
San Juan Bautista came in twenty years,
And settlements grew slowly in the land.

While France, a long time angered by the line
Of demarcation issued by the Pope,
Was finally moved, in 1524,
To send some men to this America.
Oh, she was ill content to see the new
And unknown continent bestowed to Spain
And Portugal!

                    Joliet, Marquette,
And then La Salle came southward in the name
Of France. The latter planned a colony
For France along the Gulf of Mexico.
The landing was at Matagorda Bay
On Texas' coast, in 1685.
He built a fort and journeyed through the land
In search of riches and some scattered friends.
La Salle withstood the elements, the rage
Of men, delay, disease, and dangers, end on end;
And yet, near Navasota in the spring,
Just two years after landing on the coast,
His life was taken by a murderous one
Among the men he had in his command.

La Salle was great because he found
The Father of Waters in the name of France
(The Indians called this river Miche Sepe);
And all it drained, he claimed for Louis the Great;
And, then, his Texas settlement, though small,
Established him the first white man to bring
A colony to live on Texas soil.

How jealously the Spaniards heard of this
Was proven in their urge to curb the French.
Officials met in Mexico, afraid
Explorers of the French might near their mines.
They sent armed men to fight, by land and sea;

But no one stood to meet them at the fort,
For Indians had massacred the French,
The few remaining followers of La Salle.

Yet, great or small, these once conflicting claims
Of Spain and France were destined to be used
In such a way as to confuse the size
And shape of Texas — and the flags to wave
Above her soil — for years and years to come.

The anxious Spaniards made their first attempt
To settle Texas in the early spring
Of 1690. De Leon and men
With Father Massanet, a goodly friar,
Founded missions for the Tejas tribe,
But mission matters went from bad to worse —
With Indian troubles, meager guards, flash floods,
Then drouths, and epidemics in the land —
Until, in '93, abandonment
Of Texas missions came, when priests took down
The mission bells, and buried them, and left.

Because both French and English pressed against
The Spanish settlements in Florida,
The energy of Spain was centered there,
As far as New World progress was concerned;
And, all the while, her troubles grew at home
With economic pressure, then a war,
And French King Philip, next upon her throne.

Spain lost no New World claims because of this,
But she was tired, and poor, and ill at ease;
And rest she would, but France was eager now,
Since Louisiana grew and blossomed fair,
To seek in Texas to be lord of all,
To take once more the land La Salle had claimed.

The French were even urged to it, some said,
Because a Spanish priest desired to give
Religion to the Indians, — fair means

Or less. Through competition, as he planned,
The good Hidalgo urged the French to come
For trade and mission work; and then he led
The Spaniards into vying with the French.

When Saint Denis marked out a road for France
And proved his salesmanship in Mexico
To so convince them that he meant no harm
To Spain, he was requested then to lead
The Spanish friars, soldiers, and the rest
To Texas lands along the road he marked,
And many Spanish forts and missions grew,
Since Saint Denis' *Old San Antonio Road*
Proved both a blessing and a boost for Spain.

Their San Antonio River settlement
Thrived. Some other missions then were built:
Guadalupe, where Nacogdoches is;
Dolores, where San Augustine soon grew;
San Miguel, a place in Louisiana now;
Concepcion, and forts, presidios
Protecting both the friars and their crops.
Of strongholds, San Antonio de Bexar,
A presidio De Alarcon inspired,
Was best. The mission, San Antonio
De Valero, was built close by the fort;
And this, a mission to be long remembered,
Was later known to be the Alamo;
And one, a beautious one, was San José.
Some fifteen families, hidalgos, came
In 1731 to make a town
Of San Antonio, but failed,
For all the hardships of the pioneers
Were visited upon their untried hands,
And so the growth was slow — and Spain was weak.

The French, meanwhile, were powerful in trade,
And threatened ownership of land between
The Red and the Sabine. Some spotty fighting

Flared between the Spanish and the French,
Until France ceased to be a rival for
Control of Texas when a crisis came
In Europe, and her New World claims were gone,
Upon the Peace of Paris, made in '63.

Mission after mission grew for Spain,
But failure came with many new attempts
To take religion to the Indians.
Apaches and Comanches vexed the men,
And often killed or robbed or ran away.
A new threat, England, stirred the Spanish up,
For Florida was hers in '63;
And Indians, long friendly to the French
In northern Texas, had to be controlled.
How vast were Spanish New World holdings now,
How difficult for Spain to oversee!

The tricky nineteenth century favored France
In 1800; and then, in 1803
France sold her Louisiana in a deal
Which took her from this continent again.
New Spanish settlements in Texas seemed
Ill-favored to expand. Salcedo grew,
San Marcos, next, was left in 1812.
When border and communication troubles
Paced the Texas-Louisiana line,
The Commandant General ordered such
Restrictions that the loyal Spaniards stayed
In Louisiana, while some exiled, evil,
And adventurous men came into Texas.

No strong or local politics was known
Among the Spanish colonists. They lacked
A voice of strength and of initiative;
Their close to thirty Texas mission sites
Were not enough for unity and power.
The presidio, an instrument of Spain
For military occupation, failed;
Yet Texas settlements to merit note

Were San Antonio, Goliad,
And Nacogdoches. Even so, the count
Of settlers was so low that just one town
Two thousand persons claimed — the others, less —
Or so the governor said, in 1806;
And even towns, at times, changed character,
For Nacogdoches, once deserted, came
To be reborn non-Spanish, after all;
But, even with the changes, culture grew;
And charm was found in these old Texas towns.

Anglo-Americans on Spanish borders
Pressed to get on to the Texas soil,
For they were spreading into new and fertile fields
Along the Mississippi, going west.
Then, with a grave, restraining move to check
Their immigration into Louisiana,
The authorities for Spain at New Orleans
Set up restrictions.

                    But Philip Nolan,
Adventurer of the West, was not content
To stop forbidden trade he prospered in;
San Antonio-Natches found, his plan;
And once he captured horses — thirteen hundred,
Wild and beautiful from Texas plains —
For a Spanish regiment to use
In Louisiana. Even so, he was
Suspected by a Spanish governor
Of plotting, with a crafty general
Of the United States to make some maps,
To stir the Indians to rise against
The Spanish government, and then to leave
The acquisition of the province easy
For the powerful United States.
If these were ever plans, or only rumors,
Nolan died without accomplishing
The goal. He died in 1801 in Texas
Where his party, capturing horses, met

The opposition of a Spanish force,
After having met some warring tribes
Of Indians. Even fresh for fighting,
Nolan and his fourteen men could not
Have won against the hundred soldiers sent
To capture them.

                Nolan died in battle,
But his men met other fates, for some
Were mercilessly jailed, and one was hanged;
A few escaped; and one, miraculously,
Endured imprisonment for years; and then,
With various experiments, he made
Escapes from Spanish prisons; and, at last,
In 1825, he was in Texas
As an army officer of Mexico!
And this unusual man, who told of how
A lizard in a prison was his friend,
Was hopeful, fearless Peter Ellis Bean.

Still others came, and there was Aaron Burr
Who threatened some strange plan of personal conquest,
But it, too, was destined to be lost;
While near-accomplishment was witnessed with
The expedition of Magee-Gutierrez
And their Green Flag at the capital, —
But their reprisals over prisoners
Of war were so resented that dissension came
Within their ranks, and then the Spanish army
Ambushed them, and few were left alive.

Dr. Long tried twice to capture Texas;
He, like others wanting Texas free,
Scorned the Adams-Onis Treaty which
Gave Spain unchallenged claim to all disputed
Texas land. This eager Natchez merchant
Took some local men who went across
The Mississippi, confident that they
Could run the Spanish out. The band of men
Gained members as it crossed the bottom lands

And passed by Natchitoches. Finally,
The seventy-five had doubled twice, and so
Three hundred reached the post at Nacogdoches. . .
Victorious, the band declared the land
A new republic, council governed, free;
And plans were made for featuring the sale
Of public lands. This was to stimulate
The flow of immigrants to settle Texas
Sooner than the open, western part
Of the United States. But Long, in need
Of firm support, sought out the bold La Fitte,
Who heard him through, and then declined to help.
Unfortunate was Long in everything,
For Spaniards had attacked his post while he
Was visiting La Fitte. His men were killed
Or scattered; and Bigelow's printing press,
Which published news in English, first of all
The many news sheets Texas was to have,
Was confiscated by the Spanish. Long
Was able to escape and find his home,
But he returned and captured Goliad,
While posing as an aid to Mexico
In her revolt against the Spanish throne;
Again, his men were overpowered soon,
Then Long was taken into Mexico
And there paroled; but soon he met his death.
A Mexican assassinated Long.
So went his dreams.

              A stranger story yet
Is told about Jane Long, his wife, who left
The comforts of her Natchez home, to be
A part of his adventuring; but she
Was forced to leave as soon as she had come.
In spite of this, when he renewed his plans
And met his men at Bolivar Point, again
His dauntless wife arrived to join him.
She brought her child and Negro maid, and stayed
Two years in desolation at the fort

While Dr. Long recruited men and fought.

And it was at the fort she bore a child,
The second of their union, and the first
To be delivered as a native child
Of Anglo-Americans on Texas soil.
Mother of Texas, she was justly called;
And by this title do we know Jane Long.
And it is true her pioneering spirit
Did not die when Dr. Long was killed.
She later lived in Austin's colony,
Working, serving through the tragic years;
And quietly in the Valley she succumbed,
When she had reached the age of eighty-two.

Galveston, One Saturday Night

I went to Galveston one Saturday night
And saw the waves rush in to the soft beach sand;
I heard the wind to the seawall sing a song;
Then, lo, before my eyes, they were there, right there!
And the night was filled with their shoving off
To raid a Spanish ship, to drink the rum,
And carry all their loot to Galveston.
The pirates — Lafitte — I saw them all that night
Upon the beach, when the wind was loud and strong.

I listened and waited a while, but they were gone.
Then I wandered out where the army keeps
Some gun emplacements in their solemn mounds;
And battle drab was over all the fort.
And there I paused and thought, "In all *my* life,
Not once has Texas had to make a stand
Upon her own free soil to save her sons.
These guns have never fired to hold my home.
Just threats, they are, to make America
Secure — a sort of way we use, to keep
Our powder dry." And then it hit me hard:
"How can you love a land as well as all
Those pioneers who fought out, hand to hand,
And won their prize or lost their very blood?"

"I only know I love her very much," I said,
and I felt sea mist wet my face, already wet,
And I stooped down and touched the shining sand.

How long I stayed upon the beach that night
I scarcely know; but, once awake, I saw
The pirates had returned, and *he* was there.
Lafitte was there. He counted Spanish gold;
And when he saw me standing in the mist,
He bowed as to a lady at a ball.

And then we talked, and this is what he said:
"Pensacola's powerful commander wishes
Skilled of fighters, pirate men to fight
Against America's United States,
That now the War of 1812 is lagging
For the British, heaven rest their souls, —
Thirty thousand dollars and an office
In the British army, just for me —
And I will tell you what I think of it:
I think that if my life has been a strange
And selfish life, at least I know this fact:
This treasure cove should come to be a free
And independent place, not part of hers —
Not England's and traditions she has known.
This land is young and fighting hard for life.

"I now can tell you what I plan to do.
I think that I shall see a General —
This Andrew Jackson who can whip them down —
I go to take my men to Andy now.
We'll be at old New Orleans soon to fight.
We'll wear our red bandana handkerchiefs
Around our heads and fight like hell to win.
We'll be up front, artillerymen for him,
And, by the grace of God, we'll save the land!"

And when the pirates faded from the beach,
I thought of what the history books had said
About this pirate: "scourge of all the Gulf,"
A man of plots and courteous trickery,
Who looted Spanish ships at sea for years;
While his allegiance was to Mexico,
Whose New Republic, then, although unborn,
He loved. I thought, also, of other things:
How, at the close of 1817,
The island had become a strange resort
Of desperate characters — a thousand men —
Whose depredations were too numerous.
These characters enraged our government

When they seized vessels flying Freedom's flag;
So Washington, in 1821,
Sent out a naval vessel for Lafitte.

He quietly surrendered then, and left.
And he was never seen again, until
I looked upon his face as in a dream.
That the enchantment of the isle is mine
I know with certain joy. The sunrise comes
To pour its gold upon the ancient sand.
Here is the dawn, and pirates are no more —
But just the bay, the beach, the guns, the mounds
Of greenish gray — and every promise in the sky
Of keeping ready for a nation's need.

Moses and Stephen F. Austin

Who brought Americans to Texas fields?
Who planned the contracts and the colonies?
The government of Mexico induced
Anglo-Americans to come, — indeed,
Pledged faith that those who settled on the land
Should have and keep the sacred privilege
Of constitutional liberty which they loved
And government to which they had been born.

With eagerness to bring a colony,
Moses Austin, envisioning days to come,
Arrived in San Antonio to seek
Permission to establish such a plan.
His wanderings had led him from his home
In far Missouri — on to Arkansas —
And then to Texas, where he filed at last
An application formally — and spent,
He made the homeward journey overland.
Dying from the hardships of the trip,
He asked that Stephen should be told to go
To Texas to fulfill the contract given;
For word had come to Austin, then at home,
That on January 17, 1821,
Spain had granted him his Texas dream.
He died the tenth of June, at sixty years.

His son, young Stephen F. Austin, rode
To San Antonio for final sanction;
But, meanwhile, Mexico shook free from Spain
And thus reduced the contract in its worth.
However, Moses Austin's son was calm,
And he was equal to the task ahead.

                              Stephen F. Austin
Spent hours in thought upon his father's life:

Moses Austin, son of fate's caprice,
Several times had known the sting of want.
At other times he knew a share of wealth
As merchant, first, then owner of a mine.
He knew New England and Virginia well,
And then Missouri's wilderness and mines,
Where Indians scalped the whites and burned their homes.
Indeed, the fierce Osages once attacked
His settlement, but he was well prepared
With guns and cannon, and they took to flight.
This happened when the boy was only eight,
And plans for schooling were soon made for him.

Thus, Stephen had his early schooling far
From home; and, when eleven, he was sent
To Austin's old home in Connecticut.
His private lessons from a minister
Were then succeeded by a three-year course
At the academy New London had.
Transylvania University, last —
And he was ready for the world, at just
The very tender age of seventeen.
And he was educated far above
The schooling that his father had attained,
A fact so typical of filial love
(That son should equal and surpass his source)
That it has served to make America
A land of progress; and the challenge rings
That none of us should so indulge our youth
That we will make them easy pawns of prey
To other nations fighting for a hold
Upon the freedom which we cherish here.

Stephen Austin knew his father's dream
Of colonizing Texas, and he knew
That such a dream had cost his life.
Vigorous, successful in his youth,
His father had not bowed to poverty
Which met him face to face at fifty-five

When the Bank of Missouri failed, and he
Was forced to start his business life again.
And he had left for Arkansas
In 1820, in the autumn time,
To tell his son what Indian traders said
About the Texas soil and climate. They,
Together, would succeed with settling land;
For Stephen would give up his present farm
In Arkansas, then go to New Orleans
To get the families ready for the trip
While his father would proceed at once
To San Antonio.

          And Stephen thought
How sorrowful his father must have been
When he was ordered out of town and told
To quit his plans. Then, just by chance,
A man who saw him cross the public square
Had hailed him as he reached to get his horses
At a hitching post.

          The man called out,
"Are you not Moses Austin? We have met
Some several years ago. I am the Baron
De Bastrop. I have traveled in your land.
You seem downcast. What can I do for you?"

And this chance meeting made the difference;
For, after all the plans had been explained,
De Bastrop went to see the governor,
And Moses Austin left, a happy man,
Assured that, soon, permission would be given
For him to bring three hundred families.

And Stephen heard about the homeward trip
His father made in wintertime. A letter
Moses sent to another son explained
That, if permission were allowed, he had
The applications for the colony
And eighteen thousand dollars would be his

For fees the applicants would gladly pay.
But travel overland was hard and slow.
He went by horseback over plains and waste,
Haunted by the Indians and the cold.
One day he would be soaked by sudden rain,
And then, before his hard-used clothes could dry,
A norther's sting would freeze them to his back.
He had to swim the rivers and the creeks
Or cross them on some raft that he could make,
For streams were swollen with the winter rains.
At times, a few companions stole his goods,
And he was forced to do without his meals
When rain would soak his powder, and no game
Could be provided for his needs for weeks, —
The acorns and the roots out in the woods
Became his only food for many days.

How Stephen longed to prove his father's dream!
And yet, his own life might have had a course
Far different from the Texas hopes and plans:

When he had finished school at seventeen,
He first returned to Durham Hall, his home,
To help his father smelt and process lead.
For several years he led this rugged life.
He shipped the products once or twice a year
Downstream to New Orleans. Often these
Were tedious voyages, taking many months,
For they were full of dangers when the boat
Would go aground or dash against some tree
The waters covered. There were rapids, too;
And whirlpools sometimes proved a dangerous threat.
When Stephen was nineteen, his father gave
Him full command to take a cargo down
The river to the market on the coast.
He had a terrifying time on board.
A hurricane blew inland, and the rain
Fell fast in sheets, and then the river grew
With it, and angry currents tossed the boat,

Well loaded down with shot and bars of lead.

As though it were a youngster's toy boat,
It plunged and sank — and Stephen barely made
His way to shore, which luckily was part
Of General Wade Hampton's vast plantation —
And kindness and assistance, both, were there.
But he did not forget his cargo's worth;
For, when the river fell, he loaded lead
Upon another boat and journeyed on,
Returning home by land in wintertime.

When twenty years of age, young Austin thought
Of politics. At twenty-one, he served
Missouri Territory well; and he,
Elected to the legislature, won
A host of friends, and reelections came
Until he moved to Arkansas to take
A farm. While there, he was elected judge.
He might have followed law at New Orleans,
But Moses Austin needed him, and he
Was moved to carry out their dual plan
Of taking families to fertile Texas.

Upon his father's death, Stephen Austin
Traveled on to San Antonio
And talked to Governor Martinez at length
About the colony he wished to bring.
This was in summer, 1821;
And Austin, then, was only twenty-eight.
He took the upper road on going down
To San Antonio, but his return
To the United States took him around
To see the land. The territory south
Of El Camino Real was chosen then
To be the site of Austin's colony.
This land between the Colorado River
And the Brazos was a fertile place,
And Austin's plans and hopes became intense

As he reflected on the possible
Results. Three hundred families, he thought, —
With terms that each head of a family
Be granted some six hundred forty acres
(This too, for the single men to come),
And half the acreage more to be allowed
A wife — one hundred sixty acres, then,
For every child — and even eighty acres
For each slave. His fee would come from men
According to the land allotted each.
He would survey the land, perfect the titles,
And spread the word about the enterprise
In the United States.

                              First settlements
Of Columbus on the Colorado River
And Washington-on-the-Brazos were begun
In 1821 by eager men;
And legends and accounts of them are such
That we may wonder at the leader's brave
And patient coping with the ways of fate.

When Austin first returned to New Orleans
To get his settlers, he was quick with plans.
A boat-load of provisions went ahead
To be in Texas for the colony.
When these supplies were landed at the mouth
Of the Brazos River, they were hidden well,
And then the boat returned for further goods.
Meanwhile, the colonists on New Year's Day,
In 1822, had reached the spot —
And all was wilderness, for Indians
Had stolen all their stores, so they were left
To seek wild game for food, and Indians
Posed a constant threat. The bear and deer
Were very scarce. Their hunting buffalo
Was dangerous. The mustang horses proved
To be their sustenance for two whole years, —
No bread or salt or usual foods and sweets

To supplement their diet.

                    The boat to bring
A second load of goods was never seen.
Some say this ship, the *Lively,* by mistake
Had failed to seek the Colorado's mouth,
Where first supplies were ordered to be left,
And that a number of the colonists
Refused to stay. At any rate, the loss
To Stephen Austin was a bitter blow:
Six hundred dollars for a ship, two cargoes
Of supplies, and blame of immigrants
Who left, or suffered in the wilderness.
Yet, even worse, he did not know their plight
For quite some time, for he had journeyed on
To San Antonio. He left some fifty
Men along the Brazos, a hundred more
On Colorado River banks. His plans
Seemed well defeated; and the grant was checked
By Mexican officials who had come
Into their power in 1821,
Upon Spain's fading fast in New World power,
And independence won by Mexico.

To learn his status and to plead his case,
Austin journeyed on to Mexico;
And there were dangers and expense, besides
Delays and drouth in poor near-desert land.
At that time, Austin left Josiah Bell
In temporary charge of colonists, —
And it was well, for he was eighteen months
Or more in Mexico, where he was forced
To wait a year before they heard his case —
Where parties changed in power, and politics
Constantly evoked great discontent.

His waiting time was used in making friends.
He learned the Spanish language. How he worked
To represent his colony with zeal
When the time should come that he would get to speak!

And time did come, and he was later known
As Father of Texas among her truest men.

A story told of Austin's journey down
To Mexico is typical of all
The patience and psychology required
Of him, as he was forced — time and again —
To deal with many colors, races, creeds —
And yet, remain the leader of his men.
This time, his second morning on the trip,
He felt depressed and craved a drink of coffee.
His one companion quickly urged that he
Forego the plan of making fire. They were
On open prairie, and the Indians followed
Clouds of smoke with their marauding meanness.
Austin found a sheltered place and built
The fire with care, despite the warning given.
No living creature seemed within their world.
His friend was out to find and tend their horses
Which they had hobbled on the night before,
And Austin was about to raise his cup
When a sound of many trampling horses came —
Or buffalo — and then he saw them ride:
Some fifty mounted warriors at full speed.
Comanche warriors surrounded him,
And the plundering of his camp began. He seized
His saddlebags and stood upon them fast,
His rifle in his hands. The saddlebags
Contained important papers he would need
And clothes and money for his journey down
To Mexico. A half dozen warriors
Pushed him off the saddlebags. The chief
Pulled Austin's rifle hard, but he would not
Release his grip, the while he tried to speak
Some Spanish and some Indian words to him —
And finally the message took a form
The Indian knew.

                    He was an American,
Austin said. He asked the chief if he
Was warring with America. The chief
Replied that he was not. Americans,
He said, were friends.

                    Then Stephen Austin asked,
"Where do you get your spear heads and your guns,
Your blankets and your knives?"

                    The chief replied,
"We get them from our friends, Americans."

Then Austin reasoned with the Indian chief:
How friends who journey through a land are guests
And should be treated so, and never robbed.
The tall Comanche said he was a friend
To his white brother, Austin, and he charged
His men to bring their plunder back to camp;
And all things they had taken were restored.

Despite the troubles of his colony,
Their cheers were loud when he returned to them
From Mexico. They felt security
Abounded in his leadership, his grant
Renewed and even fuller powers given.
They praised the climate — the fertility
And cheapness of the land. So many came
That magic seemed to be at work. New towns,
Brazoria and then Gonzales, grew.
Victoria and Columbia sprang up soon, —
While San Felipe de Austin, naturally,
Was made the capital of the settlements.

A man like Austin never once forgot
Responsibility. No family left,
Except a sister, very dear to him, —
And yet, he was the father of them all.
Ten years passed by in happiness and gain,
For local rules were good, laws liberal.

No doors were latched, for the integrity
Of colonists was usually known before
Admittance to the colony was given.
The standards Austin set for them were high;
And when a person proved a worthless man,
The leaders set him out and sent him on
To other parts. The moral tone was high
Throughout the bounds of Austin's colony,
And upwards of five thousand prospered there.

Other colonies in Texas grew —
And some were almost simultaneous
With his, but none approached the character
And size of Austin's, for "The First Three Hundred"
Holds a place in Texas history
Like Jamestown's settlement or Plymouth Rock,
To all of us who love America.

Other empresarios who came
Included Green De Witt, Missourian,
Who had a thriving colony, founded as
Gonzales, late in 1825.
Haden Edwards settled Nacogdoches
With a grant for some eight hundred families.
Benjamin Milam, General Wilkinson,
Robert Leftwich, David G. Burnet,
And, also, the firm of McMullen and McGloin
Soon brought thousands more, while notable
Among the empresarios were some
Of Mexican extraction. One of these
Was Martin de Leon. His settlement
Is now Victoria. Later famed,
Lorenzo de Zavala was another.

The government of Coahuila and Texas
Made eighteen or more colonial grants
Before the third year of the fateful thirties;
And Texas, then, was said to have about
Some forty thousand white inhabitants.

By now, a storm had gathered over all
The settlements in Texas. Mexico
Decreed on April 6, 1830,
A law that closed the door to immigrants.
Unfulfilled contracts were suspended, too,
And garrisons of troops from Mexico
Were to be stationed in the colonies.

A further insult was their sending out
Their convicts, first as soldiers, then to stay
As residents. Such things were odious
To Texans, ambitious for their families.
Some other hated laws — some old, some new —
Were put to test, where they had been ignored
Before the crisis came. No trial by jury
Or the right of bail was ever granted.
Furthermore, a state religion mocked
The Protestant believers. Mexicans
Raised taxes and denied men arms they needed
For protection of their families;
And, so oppressed, the colonists refused
To sacrifice their homes and liberties.

Petitioners at San Felipe met
To ask the government to cancel laws
The colonists considered most unjust;
And Austin, one of three, was asked to go
To Mexico as spokesman of the group.
He knew that dangers and discomforts would
Pursue his mission, but the voice was one
He could not well refuse. The people's cause
Was ever dear to him.

General Santa Anna, president
Of Mexico — and longing for the power
Of emperor — had little time for him
Or Texas trivialities; and so,
Defeated over constant failures, Austin
Started on his homeward trip at last.

When he had traveled nearly half the way
To San Antonio, he was arrested,
Then returned to Mexico and kept
In darkness in a dungeon for four months.
At last a goodly priest provided him
With paper and a pencil, yet his time
Was filled with loneliness and bitter thoughts.

When Austin once again saw Texas soil
Beneath his feet, he had the feelings brought
By lengthy absence past two frightful years.
Anxiety and prison life had all
But ruined his health. The colonists received
This man as one just risen from the dead.
The women wept, and ruling fathers turned
To him again for guidance and advice.

The time for war was close upon them now.
In just a month the boasting soldiers came
To take up Texans' arms. The revolution
Followed. Unanimously the soldiers' choice,
Austin was elected commander-in-chief
Of forces at Gonzales. He led men
To victories in both the early battles
Of Concepcion and the Grass Fight, which were
Main actions in the fall of '35.

But Texans needed aid to fight a war.
They needed money badly — food and clothes —
And once again he traveled for their cause,
Upon his new appointment as a man
To go to the United States for help.
Soldiers, then, elected Burleson
Commander in his stead, when he resigned
In order to obey the Texans' call.
Then Houston followed Burleson's command,
According to the San Felipe plans.

The people of America were good.

He talked to them in cities and on farms
Between New York and Louisville, and on.
As fast as men and money could be hurried
To the Texans, Austin sent them there.
He was a veritable diplomat,
And some compared his prudence and his tact
To those of great Ben Franklin in his time.

The war, a terrible and tragic war,
At last was won in 1836 —
And, even more than ever, leadership
Was needed for the new Republic's care.
The people chose General Sam Houston first,
As president, and made the capital city

     Columbia. There Stephen F. Austin,
Appointed secretary of state by Houston,
Day and night devoted all his time
To duties of the government. He worked
Without the comfort of a heated room;
And he could not endure the bitter cold,
For he had not been strong since Mexican
Imprisonment. He took pneumonia
And died soon after Christmas, at the age
Of forty years. He talked of freeing Texas
In his delirium, for Texas always
Was upon his heart.

     When he was laid to rest
At Peach Point on the Brazos, his was a grave
So simply marked by just a marble slab
That only God could know the price he paid
For "Father of Texas" recognition there.
Today, beneath a monument of stone,
So beauteously carved and so majestically
Inscribed that all who visit Austin, Texas,
Are aware of him whose spirit moved
A vast migration to a lonely land,
The body of Stephen Fuller Austin lies.

Why Santa Anna Led His Troops

No Texan could have known how many men
Were gathering below the Rio Grande
Until the early months of '36.
President Santa Anna of Mexico
Was leading them himself. His government
Was put into the hands of trusted men
While he prepared, as the commander-in-chief
"To sustain the honor of the country"
And to crush the Texans.

                    Famous men,
Distinguished commanders under Santa Anna,
Were: Ramirez y Sesma at San Juan
Bautista on the sprawling Rio Grande,
With more than fifteen hundred well-armed men;
Tolsa at Monclova, with six guns
And eighteen hundred infantry; Gaona,
Andrade, and Urrea at Saltillo,
With more than seven hundred cavalry
And seven guns.

                    General Santa Anna
Had not been satisfied with progress made
By Ugartechea, who had commanded
The military forces in the province
Of Texas and Coahuila, — or by Cos,
The general in command of all the Eastern
Interior Provinces forces.

                    And his displeasure? —
He regarded San Antonio's fall
To Texans in December a disgrace.
Ben Milam and one other Texan died
In charging his defenders who gave up
The city after losing many men.
Not a soldier of the Mexicans

COME AND TAKE IT

Remained on Texas soil past Christmas Day.
This was a bitter blow to arrogance
When added to some earlier defeats.

What other Texan actions angered him?
He knew, of course, of early tendencies
Toward independence. Even the Fredonian
Rebellion back in '26 had caused
Disquiet and unrest in Mexico.
Trouble at Anahuac and Turtle Bayou
Had followed the hated law of 1830.

Although the Texans wrote their full support
Of Santa Anna, when he sought to wrest
The power from Bustamante's government,
And helped him at Velasco, and again
In other actions, he did not intend
To give reforms they asked for in return.
He had opposed the dictatorial
Policy of Bustamante's rule
By promising a liberal government.
But, once he won, he proved a harder master
And dictator than they had before.

The San Felipe meetings angered him.
The convention held in 1833
Especially provoked his spite and fire.
Four thousand soldiers then were ordered out
"To protect the colonists," he said,
"Against the Indians." They doubted him
And organized committees of safety,
Vigilance, and correspondence, which
Continued into 1835.
Even so, the Texans would have liked
Cooperation with his government.
They pledged fidelity and would have kept
Continuance of some peaceful plan, but they
Could not endure the occupational,
Military government he sent —

Or his disbanding legislatures
And opposing governors and councilmen.

Other actions angering Santa Anna
Were early skirmishes at Gonzales
And at Goliad. Gonzales had
A cannon which Colonel Ugartechea
Had ordered Texans to release to him.
The gun, a brass six-pounder, had been used
For years as quite a threat against the raids
Of Indians. The settlers wanted it
To stay. They sent a hurried call for men
To come at once to help them hold the cannon.
By October, a hundred and fifty men
Assembled there with just their hunting rifles.
A "Come and Take It" flag was made by two
Young ladies. Defiant Texans draped the flag
Across the cannon and advanced to rout
The Mexicans. This Battle of Gonzales
Was the first of Texan victories.

Goliad, between the Texas coast
And San Antonio, had been a source
Of Mexican supplies and their good fort;

But General Cos had moved his troops to aid
At San Antonio, and he had left
Just twenty-seven men to guard the fort.
Fifty Texan volunteers were led
By Collinsworth and Milam on a night
Attack. They seized ten thousand dollars worth
Of Mexican supplies, two cannon,
And three hundred muskets. How the Texans
Needed such supplies! Their Goliad,
Thus taken in the fall of '35,
Was quite a handicap to Mexico
Throughout the Revolution. Santa Anna,
So angered by the battles of Gonzales
And Goliad in early skirmishes,

Had expected Cos to wipe the Texans out
In any action which might supersede them.

Then San Antonio! How Santa Anna
Was dismayed that Texans should have formed
Such inconsistent companies — varying
In size from thirteen men to seventy —
Loosely organized — undisciplined —
Sometimes outright rebellious to command —
And still the winners over General Cos,
His brother-in-law, now held their prisoner.

These Texans had first assembled at Gonzales
Where Stephen Austin, commander-in-chief, had been
Elected under great confusion. Then,
On October twelfth, they started marching
Toward San Antonio. They heard
Fiery speeches on Salado Creek —
Where Houston talked to them, — as well as men
Of politics and the pulpit — and the troops
Suggested that the orators go back
To San Felipe, while the army move
To make a stand near San Antonio.

Preliminary actions to the fight
At San Antonio were victories
For Texans. The first was at Concepcion.
James W. Fannin and James Bowie
Had gone to find a campsite for the troops
Of the Texan Army under General Austin.
Near the old mission, four hundred men
Attacked their ninety men. This was in late
October; and it was a clear-cut victory
For the Texans, who lost one soldier there.

The other troops with Austin soon arrived,
But he and Bowie felt that they should wait
Before attacking San Antonio.

              "Old Mill"
Was the campsite which Austin chose
While other forces held Concepcion.

Light, sporadic fighting in November
Was highlighted by the capture Travis made
Of some three hundred horses of the foe —
And by the "Grass Fight," which was strange
In all details. Deaf Smith, the famous scout,
Had galloped in one late November day,
With word that the Mexican detachment
He had seen was nearing San Antonio
With many bags of money on their horses —
Money for the troops of Mexico.
One hundred Texans rushed to intercept
The train, and others followed hurriedly.
General Cos, meanwhile, had sent some men
To aid the Mexicans. The victory
Went to the Texans, who lost not a man,
While some fifty of the enemy
Lay dead — but as for bags of money gained,
They proved to be just bags of grass for feed.
The Texans burned the grass, intended for
The starving horses in the city camps.
They kept the saddles, bridles, horses, mules,
And bags, which they so needed for themselves.

When Austin left as a commissioner
To the United States in late November,
Edward Burleson took his command.
Winter quarters rather than a fight
Was voted by a majority of the men,
Who lacked supplies of every kind, having
Scarcely a musket or a bayonet —
Only rifles and some other guns.
But, upon a deserting Mexican's word
That enemy troops were in confusion, some
Adventurous fighters wanted to be off
For San Antonio. Old Ben Milam

Led three hundred eager volunteers
Who fought guerrilla-style into the city, —
Fighting house to house and street by street
For some four days — a Texan victory —
A victory over sixteen hundred men!

So, San Antonio in '35
Had been the Texans'. It had humbled him,
The president and first of generals
In all of Mexico. He could no longer
Look to Cos or to his other men
For leadership; but he, himself, would lead.
He vowed the Revolution, which had been
So utterly distasteful on the score
Of Mexican humiliation, soon
Would change. He was prepared.

In February of 1836
His army gathered by the Rio Grande.
A mighty army — hundreds, thousands came! —
Except Urrea's command at Matamoros.
Before the month was gone, its vanguard reached
The heights of Alazan, overlooking
San Antonio. A red flag planted there
Meant certain death to every captured Texan,
For his declaration was to leave
No Texan living who had risen to arms
Against the president of Mexico.
And so it was that Santa Anna came
To ride before this troops and scan the heights
And plains below — a man of arrogance
Upon a beautiful white horse of war!

But what he did not know was such a thing
As the psychology of victory.
He thought his generals had failed his cause
When battles were not won for his delight —
So he would lead and prod his soldiers on.
He planned to force his men to make each charge

If there was not another way. This plan
Would put the cavalry behind the men
On foot. They could advance as infantry
Or meet the knives of their own cavalry.

How different the Texan will to win!
How could a Mexican, not knowing all
The spirit or the meaning of the Texan
Love of liberty, fight half so hard
For life? He had no cause before his eyes —
No cabins and no fields, no chances
For self-government. How limited
His knowledge of the principles by which
The Texans lived! In all its fullest sense
He did not know the decency of man.

But Santa Anna brought his wealth and men.
By hundreds and by thousands they came on —
The prodded soldiers and the prisoners —
The pageantry of uniforms and flags —
The scarlet flag decrying death to all
Who would defy his power in the land.
And he was there before his mighty troops —
In fine array upon a stark, white horse.

How could he fail to strike their hearts with fear?
How could he lose to scattered pioneers,
To Texas' ragged bands of fighting men?
How could he lose, indeed! How could he win?

How Texans Faced a Fateful Year

                    The Texans moved
In virtual confusion in the days
Of winter. Heroic, independent men
Were willing to defend their little homes;
But many had bravado in excess,
While understanding of their enemy
And close cooperation would have made
For better self-protection.

                    A convention
In the cold of February met
At Washington-on-the-Brazos. Forty-one men
As delegates assembled in a shack
Intended for a blacksmith shop when built.
Unfinished walls and windows, strung across
With cotton cloth, could not keep out the sting
Of a bitter norther or the fuss
And pressure of the trying, bitter times.
Two delegates were never granted seats,
And many differed in their views toward war
And government. Some were new in service.
Some were late. And it is thought that one
George C. Childress arrived at Washington
With a document almost complete —
The Texan Declaration of Independence —
At any rate, there were some fifty-eight
Who signed such a declaration of their rights.
These signers came, originally, from many
States: Virginia, Tennessee, Kentucky,
The Carolinas, Pennsylvania,
Massachusetts, Georgia, New Jersey,
And New York. Others were from Scotland,
Ireland, Canada, and Mexico.

On that same day, a committee was appointed

To draft a constitution. After midnight
Of a middle March day, it was adopted.
But the interim of early March
Was tragic for the fighting men of Texas,
For the men who tried to organize
And to prepare for war, and for Sam Houston,
The commander-in-chief of Texas' meager troops.

The temporary government set up
At Washington lacked power and unity;
But existing circumstances there
And shadows over all their prairie homes
Would hardly have made any group of men
Calm and confident, and of one mind.
Before their own convention, there had been
A provisional government in great
Disunity. The governor and the council
Had been locked in disagreement. Each
Had undertaken to direct the troops
And to issue orders to the trusted man
Who was, indeed, already chief in command.
People over Texas — in the middle
Of the fight — were hardly confident
In such a scrapping government.

General Houston lacked the quick support
Of their recruiting soldiers, getting food,
Supplying clothing and munitions. Why?
They were too busy quarreling to act
With firmness and conviction in a time
When almost certain vengeance was at hand.

The military leaders disagreed —
A general with no army cannot fight —
Other officers ignored the orders
General Houston gave, and lagging troops
Were often split on loyalties and plans.

Colonel Neill and Colonel Bowie tried

To garrison San Antonio with a force
Of just a hundred ill-clothed men. They pled
For reinforcements, but to no avail.
And all along, the General had said
For them to quit the Alamo, blow up
The fort, demolish everything, and move
The cannon and munitions to a camp
For soldiers at Gonzales. Houston knew
The prize of San Antonio was much
Too much to hold against the gathering force
Of vengeance coming out across the land,
But others could not see a way to give
The city up — a city they had won
And held so briefly for their very own.

Another group of valiant men — at odds
With Houston's plans — were sure that they could go
Across the Rio Grande to Matamoros
In Old Mexico and rout the troops
Which had been left in General Urrea's command.
One hundred men were all that Colonel Johnson
And Dr. Grant could muster for this plan,
But they made camp at San Patricio
While Houston was concerned with them and made
Attempts to turn them back — but they remained.

In all the great confusion of the times,
Small wonder apathy descended fast
Upon the populace. Colonel Travis,
Who had been ordered by the governor
To raise a hundred men to reinforce
The garrison at San Antonio,
Reported after fourteen days of work
That he had not been able to enlist
More men than thirty. Indifference of men
And lack of confidence in the government
Were points he cited in his full report.
The colonel knew the certain need of Texas,
For he used his personal credit up

In her defense. He wrote of sleepless days
And nights — of efforts to get food and horses
For the few who had volunteered to fight.

One blessing in the midst of troubled times
Was Texas' Navy. Her four schooners
Facilitated landing of supplies
And men from the United States; they ruled
The Gulf of Mexico and cut the line
Of Mexican supply along the coast —
And all was possible because the deal
For such four ships was passed well in advance
Of differences between the governor
And council.

        And still the people did not know
How serious the threat to all their land!
They did not know of all the thousands marching,
They had no ready funds beyond their homes
And fields. They had their chores to see about.
They waited. But they doubted it would be
A full-scale war. They had fought Mexicans
And Indians at intervals for years.

Even had they realized the might
Of the army on the Rio Grande,
They could not have been prepared for war.
They had so little — armies need so much —
They were almost defenseless in their homes;
So they held on to Texan independence
With a strong distaste for army life
And its routine of rigid discipline.

So they held on — and then the roll of drums
Like thunder shook the prairielands and hills,
And thousands of the enemy were there.
And down below, at San Patricio,
The men who planned to march to Matamoros
Were surprised by some nine hundred men,
As Urrea marched from Matamoros

On to Goliad. Some fifty Texans
Of Colonel Johnson's little band were killed,
But he and several others somehow missed
The slaughter in a miraculous escape.
The other Texans, out with Dr. Grant,
Were rounding up some horses to be used
For Fannin's cavalry. They, too, were killed
In a sudden, bloody massacre — and thus
The Matamoros expedition died.

The people now were hearing tragic news.
The convention under away in Washington
Was getting contacts. Messages were read,
And riders came with ever increasing speed
As massacres were pouring Texan blood
Across the land — and people fled their homes
Because they knew no way to cope with him —
This man who struck cold terror in their hearts.

Then, on the sixth day of their meeting,
An appeal was ready to delegates
Assembled in convention — an appeal
From Colonel Travis — his last appeal for aid:
"In the present confusion of the political authorities
Of the country, and in the absence of the commander-in-chief,
I beg leave to communicate to you
The situation of this garrison."
And then he wrote of other letters sent
To General Houston and to them the month
Just past.

              His last appeal reports the fight
From the twenty-fifth of February
To the third of March; within those days
"The enemy have kept up a bombardment
From two howitzers," he wrote, "and a heavy
Cannonade from two long nine pounders . . .
At a distance of four hundred yards . . .
During this period the enemy have been
Busily employed in encircling us in

With entrenched encampments on all sides . . .
Notwithstanding all this, a company
Of thirty-two men from Gonzales
Made their way into us on the morning
Of the first inst. at three o'clock,
And Colonel J. B. Bonham got in this morning
At eleven o'clock, without molestation.

"I have fortified this place, so that the walls
Are generally proof against cannon balls;
And I still continue to entrench on the inside,
And strengthen walls by throwing up the dirt.
At least two hundred shells have fallen inside
Of our works without having injured a single man;
Indeed we have been so fortunate
As not to lose a man from any cause,
And we have killed many of the enemy.
The spirits of my men have stayed high,
Although they have had much to depress them.
We have contended for ten days against
An enemy whose numbers are variously
Estimated at from fifteen hundred
To six thousand men . . . and I think
It more than probable that Santa Anna
Is now in town, from the rejoicing we hear.

"Colonel Fannin is said to be on the march
To this place with reinforcements,
But I fear it is not true, as I
Have repeatedly sent to him
For aid without receiving any."

Travis

Wrote of other calls for men to aid,
Of special messengers, of bitter needs,
He said, "I look to the colonies alone
For aid; unless it arrives soon, I shall have
To fight the enemy on his own terms.
I will, however, to the best I can
Under the circumstances; and I feel

53

Confident that the determined valor
And desperate courage, heretofore exhibited
By my men, will not fail them . . . and although
They may be sacrificed to the vengeance
Of a Gothic enemy, the victory
Will cost the enemy so dear, that it
Will be worse for him than a defeat . . .

"A blood red banner waves from the church of Bejar,
And in the camp above us, in token
That the war is one of vengeance . . .
Their threats have had no influence on me
Or my men, but to make all fight
With desperation, and that high-souled courage
Which characterizes the patriot, who is willing
To die in defense of his country's liberty
And his own honor."

        And at the Alamo,
Even as Travis wrote, the enemy's
Troops were still arriving. In his postscript
Travis said some two or three thousand men.
He signed his letter "Your obedient servant,"
And "God and Texas — Victory or Death."

When delegates assembled in convention
Were read his plea, some feared to stay and work;
Robert Potter moved the delegates adjourn
And hasten to San Antonio to help;
But General Houston held them back with words
That argued such an action would be folly —
Even treason. Their work, he said, was there.
The convention did not then adjourn.

By the seventeenth of March, the drums
Rolled closer; and the rumors of the blood
Spilled all about came thick and fast.
The delegates completed the document
Which was their Constitution, and adjourned.
Their families were defenseless and exposed.

Whole towns were broken up, as all moved east.
News of the Alamo had been confirmed —
The terrible, terrible Runaway Scrape was on!

But men would reconsider. Many stopped
In flight. Sam Houston and the officers
Of Texas would be staunch. The time had come
For Texans to decide the fate of Texas.
There was a solemn promise made by men —
Although more often kept unsaid then vowed —
That they would hold their land somehow, or die
Before surrendering to Mexico.

The Alamo and Its Heroes

When Texans fought for Texas and their homes,
The memory of dying men was kept
So sacred in the hearts of all who knew
The price of fighting on, that never once
Would any man forget. Indeed, the names
Of valiant Texans ever pass our lips,
Generation unto generation,
And they are not forgotten. Even yet
A school child tells you of the Alamo,
Of Colonel Travis and his little band
Who fought for San Antonio, their home,
Against an enemy so greatly numbered
That upon the first March Sabbath of 1836
Four thousand men attacked the Alamo;
And all the tired, the sick, the wounded men
Would not surrender.

         David Crockett fought —
A great bear hunter and a deadly shot —
There was James Bowie, Travis' well-loved friend, —
J. B. Bonham, Colonel Juan Sequin,
And courageous, eager Tapley Holland
Who was first to step across the line
And shout his willingness to stay and die.
Bowie, too, upon his cot, called out
To be included in the final fight;
And so it was, such men should live and die,
And, dying, be forever great.

There was a woman at the Alamo
Who saw the carnage and survived the men
Who fought unto the end. The Mexicans
Permitted her to leave. Two other women,
Several children and a Negro youth
Were also spared. Mrs. Dickenson,

A woman of great courage who had lost
Her husband at the Alamo — and some
Have written that she lost her infant child —
Went out of San Antonio to spread
The word and give advice of enemy
Procedure, strategy, and strength
To Houston and his little bands of men.

She saw it and retained her sanity,
But over and again she heard the din
Of battle; and the silence, after death
Had taken all the Texans, rang still louder
In her ears.

                How quiet the Alamo
Had been when first she saw it by a grove
Of poplar trees! She had come to visit
Her husband, Major Dickenson; and then
Before they realized the tragic truth
Of Santa Anna's nearness and his threat
Of death to everyone — he was almost
Upon them. She and others knew how Travis
Vowed to stay in view of the endearing
History of San Antonio.
He never could forget Ben Milam's death
And Colonel Francis W. Johnson's nerve.

Colonel Travis, naturally aware
That Santa Anna would seek some revenge,
Had kept a lookout stationed in the tower
Of the church of San Fernando. At sunrise,
The twenty-second of February, troops
Were sighted in the west. Over roofs
Of sleeping San Antonio rang the bell
The sentinel used in crying his alarm.
The people poured into the streets and talked,
And many fled the overshadowed town.

Travis quickly put his men to work
Before the vanguard of the enemy

Encamped the following day above the town.
His one hundred and fifty-five made plans
To ready the Alamo as best they could.
They herded fifty beeves into the fort.
They fortified the steady walls and doors.

On February twenty-fourth, he wrote:
"To the people of Texas and all Americans
In the World," a most historic letter —
Written after twenty-four hours of constant
Noise of Mexican bombardment, along
With continual cannonade. An order,
Demanding his surrender at discretion,
Had been sent by Santa Anna — otherwise,
The letter said, no Texan would be left alive
If the enemy should take the Alamo.
"I have answered with a cannon shot,"
He wrote. "Our flag still waves . . . I shall never surrender
Or retreat. I call on you . . . to come
To our aid with all dispatch . . . If this call
Is neglected, I am determined
To sustain myself as long as possible
And die like a soldier who never forgets
What is due to his own honor and that
Of his country. Victory or death."

Limited ammunition — just eight cannon!
Little other large artillery —
Food, also, was very scarce. Some thought
The food could last for twenty days; but corn,
Their mainstay, ran in short supply, there being
Just three bushels.

                    Several efforts made
By Travis to get help were carried out
By daring men who knew the enemy
Were all around. Each day the Mexicans
Drew nearer. Cannon balls were showering
Into the fort. Along with other letters
Travis sent by messenger was one,

A personal one, sent to a friend to ask
That he take care of his little boy. He wrote,
"If all is lost and I shall perish
I will leave him nothing but the proud
Recollection that he is the son
Of a man who died for his country."

Colonel Bonham made it through the lines
To Goliad to ask for Fannin's help.
Friends asked him not to try to take an answer
Back to Travis, for they felt that death
Would surely be his fate — though he
Should make the dash unharmed. (The Alamo
Was common knowledge as a tragedy
For days before it fell. For those who watched,
It seemed a living death, it was so hard
To bear.) "It does not matter," Bonham said,
As he rode out to take his last report
For Travis, even though it meant his death . . .
He made his way to safety skillfully
Upon a fine cream-colored horse. He wore
A large white handkerchief around his hat.
It seemed a miracle that he returned
Unharmed — or that he came to them at all, —
For his return was foregone, certain death!

Other messengers, John W. Smith
And Dr. Sutherland, were also sent.
They, too, returned — with Colonel Albert Martin
And some thirty-two determined men
Of the fort at Gonzales. They returned
Upon the first of March, and on the sixth
They were sent out again. The sentinels,
On seeing them, began to fire. A bullet
Felled the doctor's horse, and he was thrown
Beneath his mount. A broken leg meant death,
It seemed, but somehow Smith could never leave him there.
He pulled the doctor up behind him, making off
As fast as his exhausted, overburdened

Horse could go. After miles of travel,
They found help at last upon a farm,
But they were not to find recruits at all
Or to return, for on the day they left
The siege had ended.

Mrs. Dickenson was staunch in praising
Davy Crockett. A favorite story told
Was of how he sprang from bed when angered by
A cannon ball which struck a nearby wall.
He took his rifle, ran across the roof,
and picked the gunner off — a gunner
Ready with a light to fire again.
Another Mexican came up to touch
The cannon off, and he fell dead
From Colonel Crockett's deadly rifle shot.
And on and on, until the fifth had fallen,
And the cannon, ready charged and planted,
Was abandoned where five gunners lay.

The men, she said, had liked to tell of this —
To laugh and keep their courage up at times
Before the last hard siege. They quoted Crockett
On "Be sure you are right, then go ahead."
And what a strange, adventurous life was his!
Indian fights and floods, and buffalo,
Bear hunts, and once a long life-struggle
With a great, ferocious Mexican lion . . .
The men enjoyed Crockett's pleasant drawl.
He was kindhearted, honest, full of fun.
He had been elected in Tennessee, —
First, to the legislature, then to Congress,
Where he served for several years. And there
It was he heard of Texas and her need
For soldiers. He would go to help and fight
For her in such a struggle to survive.
He reached the Alamo and fought a fight
Unsurpassed in military annals —
How strange the way that it had come about:

Travis knew the fort could not be kept
After ten long days of sleeplessness,
Constant watching, firing, waiting there.
He called his men together. Then he said
What all of them had come to know: no man
Could be so hopeful as to think that help
Would come. Would they prefer to leave the fort?
He said that he would never quit the place,
But that anyone who wished to leave might go.
And it was then he took his sword, and drawing
A line upon the ground, he asked the men
To make a choice. All who wished to stay
With him would come across the line to die.
All of the men, save one, crossed over then —
And such a compact strengthened and sustained
The soldiers of the Alamo. Their time
Was running out, but the integrity
Of fighting men was kept within those walls.

On Sunday morning, the last day of the siege,
Santa Anna had ordered victory
Over the walls and through the Alamo, —
His troops divided into four great columns.
He had his horsemen back of them to prick
Them on, if they should wish to slow their push.

Ladders, axes, crowbars, battering rams
Were carried by the enemy who came
Soon after midnight on the bugle's sound.
The whole line moved at double quick advance,
But the Texans' rapid firing slowed the line
And hundreds of the Mexicans lay dead.
Inexhaustible, the enemy
Sent many men and guns to reach the walls
Upon their second charge to storm the fort.
The ladders were put up for men to climb,
And hundreds clambered up to meet their death.
Then ladders toppled over, and retreat was called.

Again a charge was sounded, after plans

Were studied and regrouping has been made.
The regimental bands played thunderously
The deguello, or the sign of death,
As they were massed south of the Alamo
Where Santa Anna waited on the bridge.
Now spurred on by officers, fresh soldiers
Mounted walls and tumbled over quickly,
Some to stay there prone, and some to rise
And fight. The Texans had no time to load their guns,
So long and constant was the stream of men
Who mounted ladders. Then they clubbed their guns
And fought ferociously from room to room.
There was no door of exit. Texans made
A screaming holocaust for liberty.

Colonel Travis, while standing on the wall
To cheer his valiant soldiers on, was shot.
The wound was mortal, but he rallied briefly
After falling down into the fort.
He pulled his shoulder up against a wall
To better get his breath; and while he sat,
An eager officer of Mexico
Rushed down to kill him. Travis summoned strength
The dying sometimes hold and thrust his sword
Into the enemy — and both were dead.

Bowie, sick upon his bed, at last
Saw Mexicans approach his distant room.
He raised himself enough to fire at them
And killed each man who braved to enter there,
Until his pistols and his gun were useless.
Then he put his knife upon the bed
And waited their approach, but none would come.
They shot him from the door.

                Just six men left —
Six Texans still fought on and were alive
When daylight came. The General Castrillon
Who captured them was brave and cognizant
Of bravery in others. He would have spared

Their lives, but Santa Anna gave commands.

Among the tired and bloody men was Crockett.
Castrillon knew well his history —
How he had fought the enemy before
They reached the fortress walls and picked
Them off like flies with rifle fire; and then
At last, when they had charged and scaled the walls,
How he had fought them hand to hand. And then,
When daylight came and only six survived
The enemy, this man stood stunned and wounded.
He held a shattered rifle and a knife,
And in the corner where he stood, a pile
Of twenty Mexicans lay dead. A wound
Across his forehead drenched his face
With blood.

       Exhausted, he and the others left alive
Were carried before the waiting General
Who ordered they be put to death at once.
When Crockett heard the sentence, he sprang out
To strike at Santa Anna, but a dozen swords
Prevented him. They pierced his heart and stopped
Him there. There was no final word, no groan,
But just a sudden momentary silence.
Even the enemy were well impressed
That such a vital man should lie so still.

How true the tribute to those fighting men:
"Thermopylae had its messenger of defeat,
But the Alamo had none."

The record of the Alamo was one
Of victory, despite the fact no Texan
Cries of winning it were heard
Across the land. Six hundred Mexicans
Were killed. One hundred and eighty-three Texans died.
The bodies of the Texans were piled high
Upon a funeral pyre where they were burned
At five o'clock that evening.

                                        After that,
The saddened people felt a war-like rage
When the story of the Alamo was told;
They purposed in their hearts to stay and fight,
And thus it was a victory for men.

It was a Texas victory again
When ashes were recovered from the place
And buried by a winning Texan force, —
Full military honors being paid.

Coleto Creek and Goliad

And those at Goliad —
The reinforcements Travis did not get —
How was it they were never to arrive?

As Fannin led them toward the Alamo,
They were already blocked from Travis' stand.
Three hundred strong they marched to help. One yoke
Of oxen to a wagon pulled each cannon
Of the four they took. The time went well
Until they reached the San Antonio River,
Where they were forced to hitch two yoke of oxen
To pull each wagon through the little stream.
The slow procedure, taking oxen back
And forth across the stream, was burdensome.
With water conquered, other troubles came.
The wagons were forever breaking down,
And they were forced to mend them on the way.
At last they learned the Mexican advance
Had cut them off from San Antonio,
By then a hundred miles away. No help
Could come, and food ran low; so Fannin
Talked it over with the men, and they
Decided to return to Goliad where they
Would seek a mission and prepare a stand.

No sooner had they made a safe return
To Goliad than he was moved to help
At Refugio, where Captain King was sent
With twenty-eight of his best fighting men —
And then, on King's great need, some hundred men
With Colonel Ward were sent to King's relief.
Scouts of Ward's command at Refugio
Met death, and others made a stand nearby;
But time was running out. The march was on!

Within those fateful days of early March
When Urrea led the foe toward Goliad,
General Houston ordered Colonel Fannin
To blow up the fortress and retreat
To Victoria. He was to send
One-third of the men in his command to aid
At Gonzales — and such an order came
In times of conflicting needs, and at a crisis
Following other orders — after aid
Had gone to the people at Refugio —
After news of San Patricio had come.
Fannin's men were scattered, and the foe
Was closing in when Houston's order came.

Fannin knew Refugio would be
The next in line of Urrea's bloody march.
Therefore, he had sent orders to the town
For people to abandon it at once —
Even before his futile march to get
To San Antonio. They were afraid,
Confused and frozen there, delayed;
And then, when enemy scouts were finally seen
Upon their fields, they were defenseless people.
King and Ward could not turn back the tide
Of overpowering numbers of the foe —
Some men escaped toward Victoria.

As Colonel Fannin prayed for news, the men
He sent as messengers were killed. It was
Against such treachery retreat was planned.
Enemy scouts were sighted near their fort;
So, on March nineteen, in the fog they left,
Hoping fog would hide their quick retreat.
A great white curtain hid the wagon train;
But weak and hungry oxen could not pull
Their load, so men pushed half their cannon off
And left them in the stream. Nine miles they made,
But progress, wearily attained, was slow.
Victoria seemed many miles away.

Praise God, at last an hour's rest — but on,
And this time two miles more, until they neared
Coleto Creek.

                        Enemy cavalry
Poured out from timberlands about the creek.
Fannin and his men were forced to fight
On the open prairie in a hollow square,
With teams and wagons centered in the place.
The Texan rifles killed the infantry
Which came upon them from the rear;
Their cannon sent the horsemen reeling back,
As they advanced from timberlands ahead.
While Texans were surrounded by their foe,
They fought effectively within their square —
The enemy lost many men that day.

From one o'clock to sundown battle raged.
They built up breastworks after firing ceased.
Great piles of dirt and carts were closely placed.
But thirst and hunger weakened men by dawn.
No water, day and night. No help had come —
No way to cool the cannon which they had —
No medicine for many wounded men.

Then reinforcements with the daylight came —
But for the enemy. Five hundred troops
Were added to the many hundreds there,
And worst of all, artillery arrived.
The Texan breastworks would be torn to bits
By one discharge of such large guns.
The breastworks men so frantically had built
Were of no use against artillery;
They had been thrown up as a fair defense
Against the rifles and the musket fire.

How hopeless was the Texans' plight,
How pitifully the sick and wounded cried!
So many wounded men — and Fannin one
Of them, though able to direct his men —

It seemed a useless struggle to go on.
They waved a white flag from their prairie stand,
Surrendering at last, for it seemed well.

Surrendering at last, with sixty wounded —
Seven dead — and what would be their fate?
What could it be when great fatalities
And wounded enemy troops were gathered up? —
Some three hundred soldiers, hurt or dead.

However, Colonel Fannin was assured
That he and all his men would be released
To go back to their homes within eight days.
Meanwhile, they would be treated very well.
With such a promise from the General,
The heartsick, weary Texans stacked their arms.

And then the cruel march began that day
For all the Texans able to go on —
But they were taken back to Goliad
And left in the old mission they had held
On just the day before Coleto Creek.
(It was about the twentieth of March.)
Colonel Fannin and the wounded men
Were brought into the mission after several
Lengthy days had passed — then Colonel Ward
And his men, whom Mexicans had captured
At Refugio. The church was crowded.
Even more were brought within its walls —
Some eighty men from the United States,
Volunteers brought in from Copano.
All were interned as prisoners of war.

Poorly fed and badly treated, men
Lived on, as day by day they felt the time
Of their release would come. Their dreams
Of home accompanied their fitful rest,
And hunger lessened with their plaintive songs.

They understood that they would be released

On Sunday. On Palm Sunday it would be, —
And great was their rejoicing Saturday night.
They hardly slept for thinking of the day.
Their "Home, Sweet Home" rang far into the night.

An officer at sunrise gave commands,
And soon the men were ready for the march.
Three companies were formed, and under guard
They left the fort, — but never to be free
Again. Each company was marched away
In different directions, under ever
Strengthening, heavy guard. Then after marching
For one mile, the men were told to kneel.
"They are going to shoot us now," a Texan called
As muskets clicked along the lines.
Some shouts for Texas rang above the fire,
As discharge after discharge pierced the air
Of that Palm Sunday, many years ago.

The only ones who were not put to death
Were volunteers from the United States
Who had just been taken at Copano
Without having fought the Mexicans.
But even men of Fannin and of Ward
Were not without the sympathy of men
And ranking officers of Mexico.
The Colonel Portilla at Goliad
Had written in his diary in March
Of countermanding orders he received
From Generals Santa Anna and Urrea.
He wrote that Santa Anna's orders were
To execute all prisoners at once,
Excepting those who were not bearing arms
Against his government when taken.
Urrea's communication stated plans
For treating prisoners well, especially Fannin.
"Keep them busy rebuilding the town," he wrote —
But Colonel Portilla could not obey
The orders sent by special messengers

From different sources. He resolved at last,
After a sleepless night, to execute
The prisoners. His diary states the plan
And how it worked, and then this statement last:
"There was great contrast in the feelings of the officers
And the men. Silence prevailed."

                        A few
Escaped the massacre at Goliad.
A few were spared because their work as doctors
Caused some mercy. One man lived to tell
Of a miraculous reprieve from death,
As bullets missed him at the massacre.

"The man in front of me was shot," he said.
"In falling back, he knocked me to the ground,
And there I stayed a moment; but when I
Arose, I found the Mexicans had gone
In hot pursuit of those who had been missed
And who were fleeing to the river. I ran
After them, no other likely way
Of possible escape was evident,
There being open prairie on all sides.
When I had nearly reached the river bank,
I was forced to make my way ahead
By going through the line of the enemy.
A soldier charged me with his bayonet.
As he drew back his musket for the lunge,
One of our men, unseeing, ran between
The two of us — and it was he who died.
I swam the river with many bullets hitting
The water, pattering around my head."

Some records state a score or more escaped
And that through kindness of one officer
Some twenty-nine were saved — but of the horrors
That were worst, was that of how the men
Unable to be marched were put to death.
Colonel Fannin was the last to die.
He had no wish to live, for he had seen

The murder of his men. The guard then took
Him outside to a square and seated him
Upon a bench. He was blindfolded there.
He asked an officer to send his watch
And the little money which he had with him
To his wife. And last, he asked a favor,
That they shoot him in the breast and give
Him decent burial. The officer
Received the watch and money, then gave word
To shoot him in the head. His body, stripped
Of clothing, was rolled into a ravine.

The bodies of the many Texans killed
Were placed into great heaps and partly burned.
The bones, collected after months of war,
Were buried by the Texan, General Rusk.

If ways of war are different at times,
Through man's invention or his mode of life,
A universal suffering always comes,
For every war of every age or clime
Must have its Heartbreak Ridge — there is no course
A war can take, away from that result.
We cannot ever think that war is right;
But even so, the wars that free men fight
Are never useless wars. The strife we know
Is ever with us. Let us not add more,
By sacrilege, to sacrificial fires.

Sam Houston and San Jacinto

Sam Houston,
Leaving Indians on the Arkansas,
Is going on a mission to his friends
In Texas — the Comanche Indians.
General Andrew Jackson has commissioned
Him to fight injustices for those
Long cheated of their lands — and otherwise
Abused. And now we see him riding
Glumly on a pony much too small
For him to ride. He is a man of towering
Stature. His feet can almost touch the ground
As he goes forth on such a mount. His giant
Saddle all but hides the pony's body.

He who cuts this sorry figure fumes:
"This bob-tailed pony is a real disgrace."
And what a man to find himself in such
A strange predicament! Two times had he
Been chosen Congressman, and then he served
One term as Governor of Tennessee.
His popularity might have been such
As to have made him President, some said,
But he threw caution to the winds one day
And started out to see his Indian friends.

Some years before, he had left home to live
With them. And Oolooteeka, Indian chief,
Had cherished and adopted Houston, whom
He called Coloneh. Houston, as a boy,
Had learned the ways of Indian life and lived
With them. He loved the forest sounds and birds,
The chase for deer, but most of all he loved
The reveries with nature. By the light
Of Indian campfires he had read for hours
From Homer's *Iliad*. When White Men's ways

And problems vexed him most, he thought of peace
That he had known among the Cherokees.

Now, he had visited with his friends again,
The first time in eleven years, and he
Had heard their sorrows and their grievances;
Had gone to Washington to plead their cause
With General Jackson, now the president;
And he had known the bitterness of men
In Congress, where they threatened and opposed
His views, but he had been victorious
In putting justice to the fore again.

So now, in 1832, you see
Sam Houston going into Texas lands.
His feelings are concerned with how he looks,
And he is constantly addressing both
The friends who ride part way across with him
About the figure he must cut. At last,
In desperation, one of them gives way
To him, and the exchange of horses makes
A happy man of Houston, who proceeds
With dignity and affability
Upon a fine, large horse with shining coat.
To Nacogdoches, first — then on he goes
To tend his mission for the Indians
In San Antonio.

                    A wild uproar
Is over Texas now. He meets and talks
With Austin who convinces him of all
The privileges withdrawn by Mexicans
Who shut the door to further immigrants
And place new, unjust laws upon the land
Once freely governed as the Texans' own.
And, so, Sam Houston once again becomes
Enamoured of a cause — and he is near the scene
When war breaks out. The fame he won
When fighting Indians under General Jackson
In the terrible battles with the Creeks — and then

Promotions given him some several times
Within the army of the United States,
Are things the Texans know and talk about.
They want Sam Houston as their leader now;
They want to see him as their army chief!

Upon election to the high command,
Houston starts for San Antonio.
But the siege is under way, and there
Is much to be considered — much to lose.
He stands upon the prairie listening
At sunrise every morning for the fire
To signal him from Colonel Travis' guns
That the Alamo is holding out. For days
He hears the signal, knowing they are there,
And then there comes a dawn when all is quiet.
He feels a void within, no words to say
"The Alamo has fallen."

His thoughts are blurred. The second day of March,
His forty-third anniversary of birth,
Had been a glorious day. The document,
Texan Declaration of Independence,
Had been born; and he, with fifty-seven,
Had proudly signed his name to it. As chief
Of Texas' army, he had ridden forth
On horseback to assume command of men
Who wanted freedom. He would give them all
The leadership and guidance that he knew.

Now, at Gonzales with three hundred men —
No discipline, no arms or anything —
He learns the horrors of the Alamo
From Mrs. Dickenson who comes to him
On March thirteen at dusk, the Mexicans
Having spared her life and several more.
She tells of death and grief — and says
That Sesma and his men are marching east.
Such news brings on near-panic in the town, —

Their thirty-two who perished at the Alamo
Had left Gonzales just two weeks before!

He cannot meet the forces Santa Anna
Surely has, with such a group as this!
So, Houston feels that he must act at once —
But in defense — he has no other choice.
The women and the children of the town
Are put upon the baggage wagons first,
Men push artillery into the river,
And a fire is set. They burn Gonzales down,
So there the enemy may find no comfort.
Thus, Houston plans and moves while he awaits
The reinforcements of Colonel Fannin's men.

The Texans make a crossing near La Grange,
Then near Columbus, and their number grows
To nearly fourteen hundred men (but none
Is sent by Fannin — and the mystery grows).
By now, across the Colorado River,
Two miles up, are General Sesma's men.
The Texans clamor for a fight with them,
But five days pass, and no command is given.

And then, Sam Houston hears of Goliad
While camping on the Colorado River, —
For Fannin, ordered to destroy the fort
At Goliad, some fifty miles away,
Had hesitated to obey at once —
Then it had been too late to get away.

Houston knows his troops are willing men,
But some are raw recruits, and unequipped.
He tries a desperate measure to withhold
The news of Goliad from them, but they
Have heard. By the morning hours, Houston,
With fewer than half his fourteen hundred men,
Is desolate. The others have deserted.

Again he orders a retreat. His men

Are not at ease. His officers are told
No hint of what his future plans may be.
The army camps along the Brazos River —
Those that stay with him.

                    He writes by sun, —
He writes by battle flare to pioneers,
Asking Texans to get agents to the men
Of power in the vast United States.
Especially, he pleads with Texans east
Of the Trinity to come at once. He says
He has no fear of death, but he is pleading
For a chance to have a victory.

And there are men who join him, but he
Has fewer men by far than Mexico —
His troops are miserable in chilling rains
And mud of Texas bottomlands in spring.
He often spends a sleepless night on saddle
With feet upon a piece of wood — and just
His shoulders covered.

                    Then he calls retreat —
Again retreat, and soon retreat again.
The men are muttering. Some want to take
This Houston from the post of high command.
They do not understand his strategy:
That now the Mexicans have split their men
Into three columns, he cannot afford
To make mistakes — so he must hide and wait.
If he should meet one-third of them and win,
He, then, would have to take the vengeful fire
From other sides. He must wait and keep
Them separated, lead them far from all
Their rich supplies. Just he must choose the time.
Just he must choose the place.

Houston knows that Santa Anna calls
Himself "Napoleon of the West," now news
Of victory at both the Alamo

And Goliad has spread across the land.
This Santa Anna's wild decree, that men
He finds in arms against his government
Promptly will be shot, electrifies
The people: settlers, new — and those of years.

And Houston's heart is troubled with the news
Of fleeing Texas families — whole towns —
That go in fear of Mexicans in such
A rush of exodus that this is called
"The Runaway Scrape." The people stream across
The roads and prairies going north, to miss
Invasion by the cruel Mexicans.
They carry food and furniture, and then
Abandon all when devil bandits ride
Beside them just to get the stores they leave
When falsely warned that Mexicans are near.

Houses stand deserted, some with food
Upon the table; stock untended, hungry —
Animals and chickens in the yard.
It seems that all is past recovery —
But there is one who will not bow to loss.

                              Retreat again.
The government is angry now. They send
Him letters, order him to stand and fight.
Such days as these, he feels, are hard to bear —
Such days as these, the darkest of them all —

Even darker than the day when death
Struck down his father, darker than the day
They sold their home and left Virginia.
He thinks of how his dauntless mother moved
Her brood of eight to live in Tennessee —
Five boys, three girls (the older boys had worked
The land and made the living for them all).

Even darker than the cuts he had
From friends when he quit teaching school to go

Into the army — an enlisted man —
A common soldier. He had railed at those
Who laughed at him and snubbed him in his choice:
"What have your craven souls to say about
The ranks? You do not know me now, but you
Shall hear of me!"

                              His mother soothed his pride
In those dark days. Her council proved a boon
To him. He soon became a sergeant; then,
The best drill officer that could be found
In all the regiment —

But these dark days are darker days by far —
Even darker then the day when he
Had charged a soldier to tear out his flesh,
To get a barbed, embedded arrow out.
His shredded thigh had never fully healed
And he could feel it now in this retreat —

Even darker than the day he stormed
Some Indians, a solitary man
To volunteer to General Jackson's call.
Wounded then, almost to death, he lay
In illness for two months and more. And when
They took him to his mother's cabin, how
She grieved for all his wasted form! His eyes,
Alone, made recognition possible.

Yes, dark days, all of them, revolved
Within his mind — but none so dark as these:
A month of constant, steady, sick retreat.
"And be assured," he writes to General Rusk,
"The fame of Andrew Jackson never could
Repay me for my great anxiety
And mental pain."

                              Upon the last cold day
Of March, a downpour drenches Houston's men.
The wagons stall at Groce's, near Hempstead.

Demoralized and grumbling, his soldiers camp
And there remain two weeks. Recruits come now
To bring their strength to thirteen hundred men,
But troops are difficult to discipline,
Since rumors fly again. This time they say
That Houston's purpose is to miss a fight
Again — and, altogether avoid being
In the war by falling back still more —
This time to the Sabine. His lips are tight
With anger as he writes in his report
That he, alone, planned out his strategy,
For he did not consult his officers, —
And "If I err, the blame is mine," he writes,
With utter frankness and humility.
And still he does not know the time or place
To make his one great stand. He hopes and prays
That soon some sign will be revealed to him.

Now, Santa Anna scatters forces fan-shaped
Over Texas. He thinks of sweeping through
The country in a mopping-up campaign;
Some troops he orders eastward, thinking more
Of Houston's men and their potential strength,
But somewhat tardily — for Houston's men
Are still on Groce's land as troops
Of Mexico's main army march to join
Ramirez y Sesma. On April seventh,
Santa Anna comes upon the ruins
Of San Felipe. Colonists have burned
Their town and fled, and nothing here remains
Except the smouldering frames of several stores.

A most enticing thought presents itself
To Santa Anna, often called "the butcher."
He will turn aside to Harrisburg,
Just momentarily, before he goes
To slaughter Houston's men — for Harrisburg,
He learns, is where the officers of Texas
Now reside. Burnet is president;

And Lorenzo de Zavala, long
An enemy of Santa Anna, is there —
De Zavala is vice-president.
So, Santa Anna thinks along the line
Of killing off two birds with just one stone —
But this miscalculation is but one
He makes. The troops find Harrisburg is like
A ghost town — so he has it set afire.
This is on a mild, mid-April night.
Three men are working in a print shop there,
No other sign of Texans comes to light.
He cannot find the officers he wants,
For the ad interim government has fled.

"Galveston Island?" He will go that way!
He will get his cavalry to Morgan's Point
And capture them . . . They slip away from him
By minutes in a fishing boat. He stays
At Morgan's Point (then called New Washington),
Because his scouts are telling him the troops
Of Houston move toward the Trinity.
He waits until the twentieth to leave.
By now his generals, troops, and fine brigades
Are utterly confused and far apart.

Houston, meanwhile, at the Brazos River
Crosses to the east at Groce's Landing . . .
April fourteenth is the day when Houston
Tells the Texans to break camp and march;
But, since he does not tell them of his plans,
They wonder where their General will go.
Some think that Nacogdoches is the place
He means to go, to join with General Gaines'
American Army, but the guess is wrong —
And luckily — for men would mutiny
Before they would take shelter such a way!

Houston knows his plan will have to work.
He sticks with it. A few miles east of Groce's
On the farther shore, he finds a gift

For Texans from the people far away
In Cincinnati: "Twin Sisters," they are called;
These two small cannon for the Texas cause.
The General is very proud of them.
He takes the muddy road to Harrisburg.
The Texans now advance — no more retreat.

But the march is difficult. The rains
Have made the roads and prairies very bad.
The many wagons have to be unloaded
And the cannon carried through the mire.
How glad the men become to reach the stream,
Buffalo Bayou, not far from Harrisburg —
But they are weary from the rugged march
And Houston orders that they halt to rest . . .
The men are there for just a day, while Houston
Sends his scouts to find what news they can.
Deaf Smith and Henry Karnes, triumphantly,
Bring in a prisoner — and best of all,
An intercepted bag of letters meant
For Santa Anna. Houston reads them all
By torchlight. Now we hear him chuckling there
Because he learns for sure that Santa Anna
Has not returned to Mexico, but is
With troops not far away — and better still,
He learns of their exact position —
How the Mexicans are scattered now,
With men all over Texas! This is it!

Houston talks to all his troops — at last
His heart is bared to them, and how they cheer!
He gives them orders for the morning march.
He tells them odds are still against their side
In numbers and in army stores. He says
That, likely, many Texans stand to die —
And last, but not the least of Houston's talk,
Is what their battle cry must be:
"Remember the Alamo!" "Remember Goliad!"

The sick and inefficient troops are left

On the nineteenth. This is near the ruins
Of Harrisburg — and under guard. The guards
Are drafted, and the sick are heard to cry,
For all the men are anxious to move on,
And none is satisfied to stay behind.

And that same morning, in a letter, Houston
Writes these words: "We go to conquer now,
But odds are so against us, I can only
Leave it in the hands of God. I trust
In Him and rely upon His providence."

Texan rafts of timber and of rails
Cross brimming Buffalo Bayou. Horses swim.
Men swiftly march all night beside the stream,
Down the bayou, till the morning finds
Them near the junction of the bayou
And the San Jacinto River. April twentieth
Is the day — but they must rest a while.
A halt is made at one o'clock, the morning
Just begun. The tired and hungry men
Fall down upon the ground and sleep.
At dawn a drum arouses them for march.
Another halt is called a little distance
Down the bayou. Beeves are killed and fires
Are kindled — but the soldiers cannot stay —
A scout comes flying into camp with news
That Santa Anna is advancing now —
His troops are coming up the bayou. Time
Is far too precious now for one to err,
So Houston quickly gets his men away.

He hopes and prays to reach the ferry first.
The Texans go at utmost speed and win
The race to stop the Mexican advance.
All of East Texas might have been their prize
If Texans had not blocked the Butcher's march;
For, indirectly, Texan action led
To Texas as a state — and then beyond,
Even to American ownership

Of California and the Rocky Mountain states.

But nothing risked in life is ever gained.
Old Andrew Jackson, president, soon points
To San Jacinto on his map. He knows —
And this is how he sees it happen there:

First, the setting is a vital thing —
The Texans in a live oak grove are poised
On the south bank of the bayou. Before
Their camp, a two-mile prairie spreads
Toward Vince's Bayou; south of it, a marsh;
To the left, the San Jacinto runs;
And Buffalo Bayou is behind the camp.

The Mexican camp is on the southern edge
Of the prairie, their cannon in position —
Now they fire! And this goes on one hour.
A few shots reach the Texans. Colonel Neill
Is wounded. Then a column of infantry
Approaches Texas lines, but they are sent
To cover when "Twin Sisters" open up.
The Texans do not chase the enemy,
For Houston does not mean to fight today.
But yet another skirmish after noon
Results in Texan losses of two men.

At sunset Houston's men enjoy food,
The first afforded them the past two days.
Both armies wait and take their quarters now
For passing of the night. The camps are just
About three-quarters of a mile apart.
Each army sees the other's campfires glow;
The sentinels are heard upon their beats.

At night the Mexicans throw up breastworks
Of trunks and baggage, a barrier that reaches
Five feet high — with just one opening
Along the center, and artillery
Are gleaming there, securing their left flank.

By early morning they are well prepared.
The right flank of the infantry extends
To occupy a skirt of timber on the bank
Of the San Jacinto River. Their cavalry,
Upon their left wing, has a vital place.

But Texans have not stirred, it seems.
At nine o'clock on April twenty-first,
Five hundred choice troops of General Cos
Arrive to reinforce the Mexicans,
To bring their fighting forces well above
Some eleven hundred and fifty men.
Texans claim seven hundred and eighty-three.

Houston knows of reinforcements sent
To General Santa Anna. This time he talks
The situation over with his men.
At noon he calls his officers to make
The plans for what should best be done.
They disagree about the time to strike;
But Houston sends Deaf Smith, his famous scout,
Upon a mission of significance.

At half-past three o'clock that afternoon,
The troops are ordered to parade. They move
With spirit and alacrity, and all
Assignments are well made, and privately.
(Possible within an hour's time
Because a swell of ground extends between
The Texans and the Mexicans.) Not one
Of Houston's enemy observes the way
The Texans preen for battle. Then a cry
From Houston's messenger, Deaf Smith, rings out.
He rides toward the troops; he swings an axe
Above his head. His horse is foaming hard
And covered thick with mire. The rider calls,
"I've cut down Vince's bridge — neither you
Nor Mexicans can get away this time —
Now fight for your lives." He charges them,
"Remember the Alamo! Remember Goliad!"

Houston now is ready. He will lead
His men. They make advance without a shot.
The Mexicans, taking their siesta,
Are aroused by Texan battle cries.
They quickly form into some semblance
Of a battle line, but they are heavy eyed
From sleep — and some are frozen with surprise.
A storm of bullets flies above the heads
Of marching, screaming Texans. On they come.

One ball has hit the General's ankle now
And several shots have hit his faithful horse.
Yet on they come. The enemy cannot
Reload. The Texans are upon their lines —
The full advance with never once a halt.
They pour a deadly shower of rifle balls.
They fight with muskets, and they fight with clubs
Which they break from the pieces at the breech —
For Texans, unlike Mexicans, must fight
Without the benefit of bayonets.
Houston's lines keep going, — they possess
The woodland and the breastwork of the foe.
The cavalry has charged and routed those
Upon the right, and now they give pursuit
To fugitives who run for Vince's Bridge.

A thousand times, "Remember the Alamo!"
"Remember Goliad!" The rout becomes
A slaughter. Santa Anna spurs his horse —
But men scream countermanding orders out.
Some beg "Me no Alamo" to escape
The fire, the fury, and the slaughtering
In the less than thirty minutes' battle time.
Then, Colonel Almonte surrenders those
Who have not died or made good their escape.

Six hundred and thirty Mexicans lie dead;
Some hundreds more are wounded; scarcely forty
Get away. The Texans lose nine men,

And thirty-four are wounded in the fight.
So, San Jacinto, Texan victory,
Confirms the independence men declared
On March the second, 1836.

When morning comes, a great deal must be done.
The Texans guard and question prisoners.
A man crawls from a thicket and lies down
In heavy grass. He pulls a blanket up
To hide his head, but soldiers find him there.
He wears a soldier's skin cap, soiled blue cotton
Trousers, and a jacket of coarse cloth.
They call to him to rise; he slowly moves
And stares at them. They notice now that he
Is wearing underneath his simple clothes
A shirt of finest linen, jeweled studs
To fasten it, — so he is mounted now
Behind a soldier, taken into camp
Where Houston, wounded, lies beneath a tree.
Half-dozing, after hours of shock and pain,
He is awakened by the prisoners' cry,
"El Presidente," and it comes to him
That Santa Anna is the man who stands
Before him now. His gestures and his speech
Confirm the fact of his identity.

A quick armistice, agreed upon by Houston
And the fallen president, provides
That he must order all remaining troops
Of Mexico to go without delay
To San Antonio, where they are to meet
The officers of Texas and be given
Orders of the treaty to be made.

While Houston talks to humbled Santa Anna,
He pulls from his pocket a yellow ear of corn,
Part eaten off the cob. He holds it up
And asks the prisoner, "Sir, could you
Expect to conquer men who fight their way

To freedom when their general marches days
Without real food — with just one ear of corn?"

His soldiers hear this speech and clamor for
Possession of the kernels. "Let's divide
And plant this ear of corn for time to come.
We'll call it Houston corn!" The General
Approves their plan, but asks that each
Should take his kernel home and plant it there.
"And call it San Jacinto corn," he said,
"For San Jacinto is your victory
As well as mine — and if you farm as well
As you have fought, I have no fears at all
For what the future holds for Texas' power."

The Treaty of Velasco, later made,
Provides that Santa Anna pledge himself
To fight no more, to get all troops beyond
The Rio Grande, to make amends for all
The private property removed or burned,
And to acknowledge Texas' independence.

But what of Houston's wound? His weakness grows
And he is taken to New Orleans soon.
The people crowd to meet the boat and cheer,
But he is far too ill to lift his head.
They give him sympathy and quiet respect —
For all have heard of San Jacinto now
And know the Texas army which he left
Is under the command of General Rusk.
The crowd assembled at the landing place
Is very dense, and it is difficult
To carry him ashore and to the home
Of Colonel Christy, a friend of his for years.
His doctor is another he had known
In early fighting at Tohopeka —
A Dr. Kerr, who works with him for weeks,
Removing some twenty pieces of the bone
So shattered in his ankle. Time moves slowly.

He is anxious to be back in Texas,
Whose struggle for survival is in test —
So just as soon as they permit him leave,
He takes a steamer going up Red River.

He is back home at St. Augustine
When the problems of the people grow
And a leader must be chosen soon.
His hat is thrown into the ring by friends
And neighbors who have watched him in a fight
And look to him for leadership in peace.
The vote shows overwhelming confidence
Of Texans in his judgment and his strength,
As he is chosen first president of Texas.

The troubles of his feeble nation rise
With raids by Indians and Mexicans.
The money problems grow before his eyes
But he can work to solve these things in time.

He has a way to pay the public debt;
Make peace with Mexico; stop Indian raids;
And win America to recognize
The Texas Independence. These things come
With frugal planning and self-sacrifice.

He wishes to see Texas as a part
Of the United States, but his successor,
General Mirabeau Lamar, has plans
Far different from his — yet Houston keeps
His dreams — he travels in America
And urges men to see the Texas question
And the mutual good in annexation.

While Houston talks of Texas in the States,
His life becomes involved with love, as well.
His marriage to Margaret Moffett Lea
Of Alabama is a boon to him
In personal and in public life. His strength
In the Texan Congress for two years is such

That he, alone, seems capable of faith
And influence enough to hold once more
The Ship of State intact. In 1841,
He is, again, the president.

Once more the wampum goes among his friends,
The Indians; and he, himself, in Indian dress
Goes out to them and smokes the pipe of peace.
Again, he cuts the government's expense
And works to keep his nation functioning.

His joy in seeing Texas in the fold
Of the United States in 1845,
When Dr. Anson Jones is president,
Is great, indeed. (By Texan law, a man
Could not succeed himself as president.)

Now Houston longs for rest and time at home,
But he is not allowed to rest. Election
To the Senate takes him to the East.
He serves in Washington for thirteen years,
And there are times when he is sorely tried
By lengthy speeches and the cumbersome
And tardy habits of his fellow men.
Occasionally, we see him whittling pine
Into some toys for children — his or others —
And, at times, we hear him muttering
Against long-winded speakers on the stand.

In 1859, he leaves the Senate,
Once again long ready for a rest
In Independence, Texas, now his home.
His age is sixty-five, and he has served
In public life for over forty years;
But he is not allowed a private life.

Elected to the governorship, he works
For unity in government. The fight
Is almost on, between the North and South.
The Texans start to talk secession now,

For slavery has been with them for years —
A part of all their economic life —
And there are long relations with the South
In blood kin and in sectional interests.
He bitterly opposes Texas' stand —
And now they call him traitor in the state
His diligence and sacrifice had made.

His friends and sons are not with him;
And Sam, his son and namesake, openly
Supports the secession movement in the state.
In 1861, his Texas goes
From the United States. He bows his head
As cannon boom withdrawal news to him.
He says, "My heart is broken."

                                    And it is —
He cannot go along with them. They turn
Him out of office. He can neither serve
Nor fight them, for he refuses Lincoln's offer
Of a major-general's commission
And the troops to force his state to stay
In the United States. He cannot fight.
He cannot fight the men of victories
He won in other years. He cannot see
The slaughtering. He cannot lead the split
Between the Union and the state he loves.

His oldest son goes off to war, to fight
For the Confederacy. He is for Texas,
Now that blood and home, close to his heart,
Are in her hands. He wants the happiness
Of Texas; and her welfare, uppermost —
In all his thoughts, is in his constant prayer.

But sad days and unhappiness are his.
His old wounds of the flesh, and new ones borne
Within his heart are much too hard to bear.
Once so erect and strong, he soon is forced
To use a crutch and cane. Real poverty

Is his, at times, when all his household suffer
For lack of the necessities of life.
"Sick of time . . . desiring rest," he passes,
At the age of seventy years. His words
Last said are "Texas! Texas!" and the name
Of her he loved, "Margaret."

                         His home,
His last of Texas homes, is now a shrine.
Go down to Huntsville, Texas. You will see
The old log house in all its simple charm.
The powder horn — the things he used — are like
Soft words of comfort from the past (and we
Can use such calm upon our souls in times
Like these). The shade of trees a century old,
Or older, falls upon the mellow walls
Of rustic brown. The echoes of the past
Are there — the Bible — and the strength of one
Who put his service to mankind and faith in God
Above all politics and personal gain.

"Will You Come to the Bow'r"

The men who went to battle sang a song,
A song of love, a little verse of theirs.
They sang about a bower as they marched —
A shaded bower, "shaded for you."
"Will you, will you" — on and on they sang.
With dust and sweat upon their clothes, they marched
Into their bivouacs and by their campfires
With "roses all spangled with dew." Yet little
Did it mean to them until a day
In April.

                        Go out some day to San Jacinto
Battlefield, and drive beside the stream.
As you approach the monument, look up —
Look long and see the star against the sky.
Read all the names recorded in the stones,
And look with pride upon the cannon balls
And relics placed within its walls of time.
And then go out and read the markers put
Beside the tree, across the fields, and on —
Until you hear a wind rise in the oaks.
But then, you really must stop very still.
For Houston has revoked his early order —
No dawn attack on April twenty-second —
He is calling now for men to fight
At four o'clock. It is the afternoon
Of April twenty-first. The Texan infantry
Are thrown out in a line that soon extends
A thousand yards. A cannon flanks
The line at either end. A flag is flying
In the center. To the right the horsemen,
Sixty strong, are stationed with a man
Named Mirabeau Lamar. These men will hold
The Mexicans from running for the prairie

When the charge is ready to begin.

Four men come suddenly to form a band —
A few impromptu snatches of a song
Are ringing out above the sound of feet
That march across the generous swell of ground
Until they are within two hundred yards
Of Santa Anna and the Mexicans.
This song is more to them, by now, than just
A song of love. It is a battle song.
It brings out goose bumps as they take it up.
You catch a little of it. Now you hear:

"Will you, will you come to the bow'r
I have shaded for you?" Over
And again you hear it in the trees.
And there you are beneath an April sky
Of Texas, while the green, green branches lift
With wind and lilting song of marching men.
You are, yourself, beneath a bower
Of nature's wonderment. How are you here
Beneath this bower? Who shaded it for you?
Do not forget to listen for the song
That predicated victory for men
At San Jacinto in that fateful spring
When Texans clutched a fervid hope to win,
And win they did. Oh, who can hear it now
More clearly than you hear it in the trees:
"Will you, will you, will you, will you
Come to the bow'r?"

Under the Lone Star Flag

Of the many sympathizers known to Texas
From her neighbor, the United States,
A few stand, colorfully emblazoned
On the pages of the Texas Past.
Supplies had come from eastern valley states
Of Old Man River, and some from New Orleans.
Donations and investor's loans were made
Throughout the land. Recruiting stations were
Set up in Cincinnati, Louisville,
And New Orleans. Well known as fighting men
Were the "New Orleans Greys." Alabama
Sent the "Mobile Greys" and her "Red Rovers."
A Georgia battalion in 1835,
Came into Texas with a flag new-sewn
By Johanna Troutman. Fannin flew
This flag at Goliad, and after that
It came to be, with its one star, a guide
Toward freedom: the one thing worth fighting for!

With that freedom won, it flew for years
Above the new Republic, having been
Officially adopted as the standard
By Congress in the year of '39.

Some say the first flag had a single star
Of gold upon an azure field. We look
Upon the Lone Star flag today and know
A lot of living and the history
Of Texas ripples in its folds of red
And white; while in its field of blue,
The one white star of freedom shines.

A lot of living! Yes, it watched the years
Of struggle and of gain. It watched the people

Joyfully return to land they left
When frightened into joining in the flight
Of the Runaway Scrape.

                But still there was
A battle for the right to live; the pledge
That Santa Anna made became a worthless vow.
Internal troubles, too, beset the men
Who tried to lead the government with care.
The policies of presidents were not
The same. The men who steered the course of Texas —
First, Sam Houston, followed by Lamar, —
And then, again, the trusted Houston served, —
And last of the three Texas presidents
Was Dr. Anson Jones, whose office saw
The passing of that office and the birth
Of Texas as a state, — even though
His personal views were somewhat different
From those of the pro-annexation men.
It was the best, at last, for all concerned;
And so the new Republic came to be
The state of Texas in America.

But more of those nine years between the time
Of San Jacinto and the closing date
Of the Republic!

              David G. Burnet,
Provisional president, and other men
Who served as officers, were those to write
The Treaty of Velasco and to make
Disposition of the president
Of Mexico — some wanted death for him.
Civil authorities and army men
Did not agree on many things of state.
The army's Major General, appointed,
Was Lamar — the Major General, elected
By the men, was General Felix Huston.
And the army had its way! It grew
In rowdiness and numbers; but, until

Houston saw a way to slow it down,
The civil officers refused to move
Against its strength. They had some lingering fear
Of interference by the Mexicans.
Impending trouble was not unprovoked,
For some provisions of the Velasco treaty
Had not been promptly championed. By its terms,
Defeated Santa Anna was agreed
Permission to return to Vera Cruz.
He was to use his power to secure
From Mexico her recognition of
True Texan independence. His troops were out
Of Texas by mid-June — but he was not,
For bitter controversy over him
Ensued until November. Houston, then
The president of Texas' new Republic,
Sent Santa Anna on to Washington
For conferences with Jackson. Finally,
He was permitted safety into Mexico.

The Texas Navy added color soon.
Back in the Texas Revolution, there
Had been four vessels: the *Invincible,*
The *Brutus,* the *Independence,* and the little
Liberty — and how their men could fight!
Just four small vessels, but they made their mark
In harassing enemy commerce. Many say
They helped to keep the Mexican blockade
Of Texas ports from being less then half
Effective. One was captured in the war,
And two were wrecked soon after fighting ceased.
The young Republic, left with just one ship,
Feared a real blockade of Texas ports
By the navy of the Mexicans;
So, the government bought other ships —
Some six or eight — from the United States,
And sent them out to prey along the coast
Upon the Mexican commerce. This proved
Good sport for men whose commodore

Was Edwin W. Moore, a former Navy
Officer of the United States.

Tabasco, Yucatan, and other towns
That stretched along the coast of Mexico
Were captured. The Navy's last expedition
Was about the middle of the year,
In 1843, when it returned
To Galveston. It had kept the ports
Unhampered, free to operate, — but then,
It often went against the orders given.
President Houston officially declared
The whole fleet to be pirates at one time,
But this was under stress, — and it would seem
The Texan commissioners were more inclined
To praise than to rebuke the commodore.
Some four ships of this Texas fleet were held
To be included in the nation's fleet
When annexation came in '45.

One thing which gave a boost to government
When Houston first was president of Texas
Was the creation of the General Land Office, —
For Texas was endowed with bounteous land,
Upon the one hand, while her many debts
Were piling skyward on the other. Houston
And the Congress passed the "Homestead Law"
Which still exists today. It stipulates
That the homestead of a family cannot
Be taken for its debts. This, along
With other phases of the law, induced
A rapid settlement of Texas lands.

But even this new office had its strife
With widespread frauds; forged paper for land scrip
Was found in circulation. Yet, it seemed
That progress overshadowed setbacks soon,
For empresarios were coming in
With good results. Henry Castro brought

Six hundred families to settle west
Of San Antonio. These Alsatians
Founded Castroville, a quaint landmark
In Texas of today. Near present Dallas
Was the W. S. Peters settlement, which came
To be the backbone of the Cotton Belt.
The Fisher and Miller enterprise induced
Prince Carl of Solms-Braunfels and his caravan
To come to Texas. Later on, some several
German settlements were made. And countless
Numbers of Americans soon flocked
To Texas. Good or bad, they came!

                              Lamar,
The second president, gave dignity
To education with a vital plan —
To quote his words: "the cultivated mind
Is the guardian genius of democracy . . .
It is the only dictator that freemen acknowledge
And the only security that freemen desire."

His other policy was his belief
In a successful military strength
Against the Indians and the Mexicans.
He used both the Army and the Texas Navy
In his plans against the Mexicans.
But dark, indeed, were some results of this, —
Most notably the Santa Fe Expedition.
And, against the Indians, was a plan
That brought about the regrettable Cherokee War.

He only knew the resolution passed
By the first Congress under President Houston.
Its terms declared the western boundary
Of Texas as the Rio Grande from mouth
To source and thence due north as far
As the forty-second parallel, and so
He wanted to preserve the terms set down.
Lamar could not foresee the ways

His policies on paper would become
Involved with repercussions and mistakes.
He knew the Texans had been sorely tried
By Indian brutalities of tribes
Along the west — and by the cruelty
Of Mexicans along the borderlands.

The Linnville Raid of 1840 proved
The greatest single raid of Indians;
They swept, one thousand strong,
Down the broad Guadalupe Valley, killing,
Sacking homes and stores, and stealing horses

Until an army of Americans
Defeated them in the Battle of Plum Creek.
These Comanches and some other tribes
Continued intermittent Indian raids,
But soon the White Man carved a new frontier.

Houston, back in the reins in '41,
Restored at once a friendly policy
Toward the Indians — but not again
Toward Mexico. Too much had happened there,
Aggressively, to be forgotten soon.

The Mexicans most suddenly appeared
In 1842; they took the town
Of San Antonio — and others, too,
Including Goliad, Victoria,
And Refugio; and then that spring, before
An army could advance upon their troops,
The enemy retired to Mexico.

They came again that fall, recapturing
San Antonio. They left as soon
As Texas Rangers and defenders came,
But this time fifty men out of La Grange
Were rounded up and killed most ruthlessly.

The public sentiment in Texas soon

Became so heated over this, that men
Were eager to pursue the Mexicans.
The country, on war footing once again,
Assembled men at San Antonio.
General Somervell led Texas men
Toward the Rio Grande, but orders changed
Against invasion. Forces then were ordered
Back to Gonzales to be demobilized.
Three hundred pushed ahead, with Colonel Fisher
Leading them to Mier in Mexico.
Two thousand Mexicans defeated them
And marched them off as prisoners of war.

Ironically, the Texans almost won
At Mier, but they misjudged their fighting skill
And surrendered to large enemy forces there.
As prisoners of war, they mutinied
And escaped, but after almost starving
In the mountains, they were finally captured
And returned to the authorities
Who executed one of every ten.
This was determined by the men who drew,
Blindfolded, beans of black or beans of white,
The black beans symbolizing death at once.

The other prisoners were marched away
To Mexico City and imprisoned there
In the dreaded Castle of Perote.
Eight men escaped the horrors by a break
For freedom. Others were kept half alive
For many months before they were released.

Ironically, again, a mission led
By Colonel Jacob Snively prospered
In its interception of a train
Of richly laden wagons on the way
To Santa Fe. There Texans won a fight
Against the Mexicans, — but just in time
To be opposed and then disarmed by forces

Of the United States. It was alleged
That Texas troops had fought upon the soil
Of the United States — then neutral ground.
The incident was one of several fights
Along the border. Strangely, some years later
The government acknowledged that its troops
Were outside the United States and paid
The state of Texas liberally for arms
Which Snively's men had given up to them.

Government in the Republic showed
At least three unique episodes to note:
The first was called the Council House Fight.
This followed on the heels of what had been
A peaceful plan to settle differences
With the Indians in their land disputes.
The leaders of both sides, it was arranged,
Would meet at the assembly taking place
At San Antonio in 1840.
The Indians were to bring white prisoners
For exchange and to make future plans,
Since much sporadic fighting had occurred.
However, only one white prisoner
Was brought. Comanches, numbering forty braves
Along with a dozen of their Indian chiefs
Were then detained and held as hostages
When Texans saw their one white prisoner
Of war. This effort to make council work
A way of settling differences of men
Resulted in a fight. When it was stopped,
Few Indians were left alive; several
Women, among the Texans, lost their lives.
It proved some strength in Texas dominance;
But as a council, bloodiest defeat.

The strangest situation came about
Some two years later. This episode, a comic
Opera incident of history,
Is often labeled as the Archive War.

The Mexican invasion brought it on,
And, since it ended well, no tragedy
Of disagreement spoiled the government.
In point, it hinged upon the proper place
To make and keep the Texas capital.
In 1839, the site of Austin
Had been chosen — this, despite the bleak
Frontier position it then occupied.
The government commission chose this site
Although the fight for Texas Independence,
Which had been a victory of note
In 1836, had not insured
The safety and the recognition planned
And hoped for by the Texas government.
Some foreign nations and her greatest neighbor,
The United States, had recognized
The new Republic as a nation free
From Mexico — but Mexico had been
Reluctant to admit defeat or give
The reassurance Texans thought they won.
When Mexicans came back in '42,
The seat of government was moved at once
To Houston by the Texas president.
It had, at one time, been the capital.
The citizens of Austin felt that he
Might want to keep it there. The city bore
His name, and some concluded that he felt
Some partiality, which they opposed.
The Austin citizens blocked such a move
By seizing all state papers at that site
And holding them. The president of Texas,
In December, sent a company
To seize the archives of the government,
But his small force had little real success.
They loaded wagons partially and fled,
Pursued by Austin citizens who forced
Them back to Austin. Shots were fired, and words
Flew hot and fast, but men and documents
Survived the spree. The Texas president

Removed the archives to another place;
Washington-on-the-Brazos, it was called;
And for a time, it was the capital.
Then, in 1844, the seat
Of government was finally returned
To Austin under President Anson Jones.

Land problems caused another episode.
A tragic yet a local fight arose
In Shelby County — and in Harrison.
It assumed proportions of a war
Of civil strife, in which some thousand men
Were soon engaged. Two armed camps fought it out,
The "Moderators" and the "Regulators"
They were called; and for about two years,
A vendetta prevailed, and fifty men were slain.
Courts ceased to function. Families were distraught.
President Houston had success in quieting
The disturbance in 1844,
But ill effects and bitterness prevailed
For years.

              Financial troubles had beset
The new Republic from its origin:
The president's "log mansion" had two rooms,
His meager salary most slowly paid,
His personal note was given to supply
Necessities for early government.
Of all financial expedients
Resorted to — tariff, tonnage dues,
Port fees, property taxes, business taxes,
Land sales and dues, and poll taxes —
All were not enough to clear the debt.

In fact, the government began in debt;
But the Republic's short ten years of life
Increased this debt eight-fold. The money system
Of the government was never good.

Expenses rose; collections rated poor.

No specie was obtainable. The war
Incurred expense beyond the people's power
To pay, — the military policy
Of Lamar was even more beyond
Their means.

                        In 1844, the last
Of Texas' national elections brought
A man of wisdom and of compromise
For Texans in their transitory hour.
Anson Jones, as president, devoted
Time to issues of the government
Involving annexation, and he worked
To wind up all affairs of the Republic
With efficiency and clarity of terms.
Dr. Jones had served the new Republic
As Houston's secretary of state, and now
One hundred twenty thousand Texans looked
To him for guidance. Their Republic, dear
To them, had long since won from foreign powers
A recognition of its government.
And Mexico, at long last, had been moved
To sign an armistice in '44;
But their reasons for, and the results of such a move
Were questioned; and although the new Republic
Still was loved, the annexation answer
To their problems seemed the best.

                        For years
The Texans by a large majority
Had been for annexation to the United States.
The subject of annexation was submitted
At the first election ever held
In the Republic, and the vote for it
Was favorable, almost unanimous.
As for the States, the South was favorable
To annexation from the start — opposed
Were many states of antislave sentiment.
And, strange to say, the question was involved
With foreign countries — not just Mexico,

But France and Britain, whose investments were
To be protected at a price to them.
These nations were most anxious to prevent
The annexation of Texas as a state.
A scheme in London, by which the British dealt
With a Mexican representative,
Involved Mexican recognition of Texas
And her boundaries. The deal, in point,
Was planned in order to protect investments
Of the British, made in Mexico.
It offered Texas guarantee of borders
And of freedom by their dual support.
Texas was to assume five million dollars
Of the Mexican national debt, and she
Would then be favored with complete accord.
The scheme was never carried out, because
Upon the heels of this decision, came
A change in plans by Britain; now
She thought of politics affecting her
In the United States, where issues grew
Around the annexation question coming
Up in the United States campaigns
For President in 1844.
Deferring action on the Texas question
Seemed in order to the French and British,
For Americans resented England
And would surely fight an English plan
Of interference on the question now.
Polk, elected President, was pledged
To Texas' annexation; but before
Inauguration Day the choice was made
By the Congress. By March of '45,
A joint resolution annexing Texas
Was passed. The Texas President, Anson Jones,
Was challenged thereupon by men of France
And Britain to agree to withhold action
For some ninety days, while Captain Elliot
Hurried down to Mexico to ask
That they recognize the Texans' freedom,

Provided Texas never join the States.
This strange maneuver then gave Anson Jones
The right to ask the Texans of their choice
Between a safer national plan of life
Or annexation to the United States.
And this he did — and they decided well.

While Texas, as a nation, never had
A heavy role in world affairs or plans,
Her annexation to the United States
Brought forth some repercussions and a war
With Mexico, albeit, earlier —
And all along — there was a bond of strength
Between the Texans and the Americans.
American Presidents and diplomats
Had looked at Texas longingly, and with
Some rights, as treaties were interpreted
In ways to make their claims seem justified.

Who owned this vast and fertile Texas land?
President Jefferson was sure that Texas
Was to be included within the bounds
Of the Louisiana Purchase. Others, too, —
John Quincy Adams, who sent Henry Clay
And Joel Poinsett to Mexico, was one
Who worked for holding it, but had no luck.
When other plans had seemed to fail, a scheme
To purchase Texas from the Mexicans
Was tried in vain under Andrew Jackson.
The offer of five million dollars was not found
Attractive, or the minister whom Jackson sent
Did not prove capable of handling it.
Perhaps the Mexicans suspected threats
And politics involving Texas lands —
Even as the revolution flared —
For it was known to them how Houston
Was a friend to Jackson, — and the two,
In different capacities, had long
Been anxious to have Texas join the States.

As for the Texas Independence won
At San Jacinto, the United States
Was glad and proud. Both houses of the Congress
Had, in March of 1837,
Voted recognition — and a move
Had then been made by Jackson, sending first
La Branche, as charge d'affaires to Texas,
To arrange an early annexation.
Such a move as this had been encouraged
By Houston's sending William H. Wharton out
As minister to the United States
When Congress had been somewhat slow to see
Advantages of recognizing Texas —
Which was a ticklish question, politically.

Delays were then occasioned by the change
In presidents and party policies,
As well as by slow steps taken with Mexico.
Van Buren had become the President
In a trying time of panic in the land —
In times of animosity of men,
Of states, of sections of America,
Concerning slavery and its related
Issues. He was not at all atune
To hear the annexation offer, framed
By President Houston late in '38.
A stalemate came, and nothing more was said
Between the governments for several years.

And then the picture brightened with the glow
Of economic values Texas held;
And even glints of jealousy were there,
As England looked with interest at the fields
Of Texas cotton — but Mirabeau Lamar,
New Texas President, had other dreams
For Texas, and he moved against a plan
For annexation.

                         This intensified
The drama and the nation's interest

In Texas. Fear of England rose again
About the time of President Tyler's term.
Increasing difficulties — such as Houston's
Feigned indifference and the death of Upshur,
Who had been appointed to reopen
Talks with Texas — slowed the plans again.
Even Carolina's John Calhoun
Could not obtain the Senate's needed vote
To make a treaty hold in '44.
This treaty, so rejected, has a point
Regarding tidelands of the Texas coast.
Look back and see the terms which entered in:

Annexation would admit the land
Of Texas as a territory, first;
And second, claims of the United States
Would make the nation in complete control
Of all the Texas public lands; and third,
The nation would assume the Texan debts
Of government. This was the treaty scorned
By the Senate in America.
(How can it be they seek the tidelands now!)

The Texas question had a major role
In politics in 1844.
James K. Polk was bold enough to say
He wanted Texas in — and Oregon —
And so he won the Democratic nod
For candidate — and then the Presidency.
This, over popularity of Clay,
Whig candidate for President, and others
Who would lead in keeping Texas out.

While President Tyler long had wanted Texas —
And his plans had failed — the Congress saw
The wisdom of his plea, as Polk
Advanced into the nation's Presidency.

Men moved by Tyler's annual message read

In December '44, soon followed him
In his suggested plan for annexation.
The terms of his treaty were to be
Embodied in a joint resolution,
Since this would serve both Houses in appeal
And interest, and would hardly fail again —
Requiring only a simple majority
Of votes in each of both the Houses; while
A treaty, otherwise, would risk defeat.

Taking up the joint resolution
As a quick procedure, Congress passed —
With its own terms — a final plan in March.
This resolution differed from the treaty
Of annexation in some several ways:
Texas was to be annexed as a state —
It was to keep its public lands, instead
Of giving them to national control —
It was to pay its public debts itself —
And it could later be as many states
As five (if it should ever wish to so
Divide itself) provided that the state,
Or states, found lying north of 36° 30'
Should be free.

       But Texas' public lands,
Remember, were to be her very own —
And, in a sense, she bought them at a price,
For she would pay her own great public debt —
And so, the tidelands came by solemn terms
To Texas, as she became the twenty-eighth state.
And President Tyler signed the resolution
On the very day the Senate's vote
Approved it.

       Major A. J. Donelson
Was soon in touch with President Anson Jones,
Of Texas. Jones had not foreseen the wave
Toward Texas coming up so suddenly;
And he had not used "annexation talk"

In his inaugural address, or other
Messages. To complicate things more,
The treaty had been signed with Mexico,
Whereby the Texans would retain their form
Of government for recognition of
Their independence won from Mexico —
Such independence to be guaranteed
By the British government, as signed.

The people's choice was asked by Jones who knew
That annexation, likely, would mean war
Between the United States and Mexico.
On the fifteenth day of May in '45,
He summoned a convention for July.
The delegates of Texas should decide
Along with the Texas Congress, called to meet
In special session earlier. The Senate
Changed by June, the twenty-third,
To go unanimously in favor of the plan
Already favored by the House. July
Saw eager delegates to the convention
Adopt an ordinance by which they would
Accept the terms of annexation — only one
Dissenting vote was made; and then they framed
A constitution, ratified that fall,
The thirteenth of October; and by winter
All was done except the final step.
The Congress of the national government
Accepted Texas' constitution late
In December '45. The twenty-ninth
Has been declared, officially, the day
Of Texas' entrance into the United States.

The final ceremony Texas made
On Texas soil was held in February
Of 1846. The salvos boomed
From her historic cannon,
At the young Republic's exodus.
The people cheered the State of Texas in,

But there were tears for her Republic
As the Lone Star flag came down
Amid the fighters and the pioneers who loved
That single star. It had been bought with blood,
With prayers for freedom, with the constant toil
Of men and women — in the forts, on farms,
On waters, or wherever Texans fought —
In good days and in tragic, tragic hours —
But now they lowered it, and in its stead
They placed the banner of the Stars and Stripes
Of the United States. And Anson Jones
Stood watching this and said, "The final act
In this great drama is now performed:
The Republic of Texas is no more."

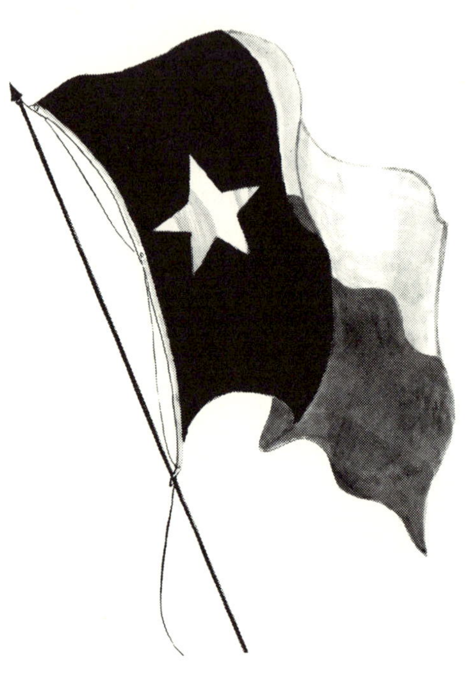

The Drawing of the Black Beans

No freedom, it would seem, is static fact.
It must be daily watched, defended, worked for,
And preserved — or it will soon be gone.
The trends of thinking men have not been clear
As to this premise in our national life.
There have been times when ideologies
Were used, though well intended, by idealists
To put a blindfold of soothing velvet
Over tired eyes to hide the truths
Of stark reality and the sufferings
Of humanity. This was not good.
These men took heartbreak out of war.
They said to leave it out of history books
Because the precious youth we have today
Should not be stirred by horrors done to man.
They said that war had had its day and gone,
And that the world, safe for democracy, would be
A place in which to have Utopia.
If peace were talked, and taught, and lived, they said,
We could forget the prison camps, the deeds
Of enemies, and all unpleasant things.
Deleted pages from the history books
Were soon replaced with pleasant, friendly ties
Between the nations — and the thought was good
Behind it — but the evil of it all
Was in the carefree attitude it made
Among our young. We came to have a false
Security. We thought that only heathens
Of some dozen centuries ago
Were barbarous. We had no thoughts of war
Beyond its pageantry. We did not know
Of torture in a modern world. We had
No faint conception of the strategy
And trials of the men in great campaigns.

We could not value all our privileges
Because we were not taught the asking price
By which they came. Our lives then grew in years,
But not in knowledge. We avoided polls
If lines were long — our birthright thrown aside
Because we were not glad enough to have
The right to cast a vote. We lived in ease
And let a Hitler rise. We went to fish —
And let some alien Communists move in.
It would be well to see the cost of war.
It would be well to know sadistic trends
Of officers and men in battle. Surely,
Surely, not to breed that prejudice
Or hatred of another land or race,
Which would contaminate the world, but rather
To see needs for fair and decent moves,
To know that consequences follow wrongs
Of men, to know that human flesh and spirit
Can endure by lessons from the past,
To better value what we have and hold.
To better love a God of greatest love —
But to be mindful that He, too, can be
A God of vengeance and a God of wrath.

If we look back to 1842
With Houston as the President of Texas,
We can see the people enjoying peace,
Their independence won some six years past:
But peace was not to last, for Mexico
Was moving troops toward Texas once again —
Again to San Antonio, with hopes
To take the city and to rule the land.
More Texan blood, it seemed, would surely flow.
But autumn time had come to prairielands,
And with the autumn, strong resistance came.
The Rangers, militiamen, and volunteers
Would strike invaders from the Texas soil.
And soon it was that General Adrian Woll,
After losing some one hundred of his men,

Took his remaining army back across
The lazy Rio Grande. But he had angered
Many Texans in recapturing
San Antonio and in the murder
Of the fifty Texans from La Grange.

Against the orders of the government,
A band of Texans under Colonel Fisher
Took the war beyond the Rio Grande.
While they were mutinous in their advance,
They were convinced defensive war was wrong;
They had borne invasions, time and time
Again. Now the humility of seeing
Soldiers in their streets, entering,
Perhaps, their homes — and threatening to come
Again, so stirred them that they could not stop.
They wanted war in other streets. They wanted
War on other land. Was not the soil
Of Texas soaked enough in blood and tears!
They would go on, as ordered first to go
By Houston — who had later felt restraint,
Expressed through his discretionary orders
To Somervell, who could proceed as he
Thought best. They were so close to Mexico
There seemed no turning back. Their hearts were set
Upon offensive battle. Thus it was
That their three hundred men who went across
Encountered an enemy of twenty hundred
At the little border town of Mier
In a blowing rain on the night of Christmas Eve.

Ampudia, the Mexican general,
Was ready to receive them when they crossed
The river. They had avoided guarded fords,
But clambered down steep banks and waded
Through the cold, dark waters to the side
Of Mexico. They kept their powder dry
And it was needed as they made the bank
Before the city. But they saw their fighting

Count a quick retreat for Mexicans
Who came again by many companies more.
The Texans pressed toward the city, fighting
Ever gathering forces of the foe
Until they finally pushed their way to Mier.

Of all the strange phenomena of war,
The story of the cannon was unique.
The Mexicans had cannon in the street
Of Mier. They were well planted to keep up
A raking fire against the fighting men;
But the Texans dodged around the corners
When they fired, then when the balls had passed,
They would jump out into the street and shoot
The gunners down. It served to win some ground.
A row of strong stone houses soon was theirs
After they had battered down the doors,
And from those walls the Texans kept up fire
Against the enemy. Some ragged holes
From which to shoot had first been made by axes
And by crowbars. Then the Mexicans
Took to the housetops and returned the fire.
This was the first the Texans really felt,
But they fought on until the midday came.
It was at noon a large white flag was seen
Coming from the lines of Mexico.
The Texans screamed for joy on having won,
And felt that Ampudia had quit the fray.

But such keen joy was not to last for long.
Their Colonel Fisher went outside to meet
The bearer of the flag who brought a note:
The message from the General was frank.

It would be useless to fight on, he said.
They had great numbers, and eight hundred more
Fresh troops would soon arrive. A promise given
Warned against more bloodshed and said Texans
Should surrender, that they would be treated

Well and would be exchanged for some prisoners;
That if they did not surrender, every man
When captured would be put to sudden death.
Five minutes was the time allowed to Fisher
In which to see his men and send his plans.
He drew the men into a hasty line
And gave advice that they should give up arms.
The General was reliable, he felt —
He had once dealt with him before in war —
He could be trusted to exchange them soon
As prisoners of war. Surely they
Would be in Texas by spring planting time.

At first the men resisted this advice,
Remembering the Alamo and Goliad;
But some were ready to surrender soon,
And they marched over and laid down their arms.
Then others followed, and in time some more
Until the whole of Fisher's army moved
To bow their heads as prisoners of war.

The promise of the General was forgotten.
He kept them in some stuffy rooms for days
Then he put heavy irons on their hands,
Tied them up in pairs, and set them out
For Mexico City, a thousand miles away.
The Mexican soldiers carried fixed bayonets
Behind them as they marched through Mexico.
Sore feet and thirst were horrors of the march,
And when at night they hoped to get some rest,
They were deprived of blankets and forced down
In filthy cow pens. Fires were burned to keep
The cold north wind from killing them,
And when the fires burned down, they raked away
The burning coals and lay upon the ashes
To get warm. But when a town was reached
They were marched around the square and through the streets
Like circus animals on dress parade.

The Texans stood the march for six long weeks.
They talked to keep their spirits up. They planned
Escapes and tried to keep from losing heart.
Finally their chance to move arrived
At Salado on a winter's day
In 1843. They had reached
A farmhouse where they rested some at night,
Then, with the sunrise, they surprised their guards
Who were at breakfast. After taking guns
Of those inside, they scattered soldiers waiting
In the yard. They took their guns and horses
And were fast upon the road for home.

But they grew fearful of the open road,
Of being followed and recaptured there,
So many miles from home. They did not know
The country, and no guides were there to help,
So they went to the mountains for relief.
It was this choice that brought more suffering,
For they were lost for days and had no food
Or water. Tongues were swollen. Men were crazed.
They killed and ate their horses. Then they walked,
But they were weak and powerless to go
For more than just a few steps at a time.
They threw away the guns they could not hold
In weak and useless arms. And while they seemed
Like dead men walking, their recapture came.

The band of Mexicans who captured them
Was led by General Mexia. Although
They were his prisoners, he pitied them.
He always treated prisoners well. The men
Were given food and water, and the sick
Were tended well. They marched again, when well
And strong enough to go to Salado.

But once they were within the prison walls,
An order came from Santa Anna's office
As a terrible decree of death.

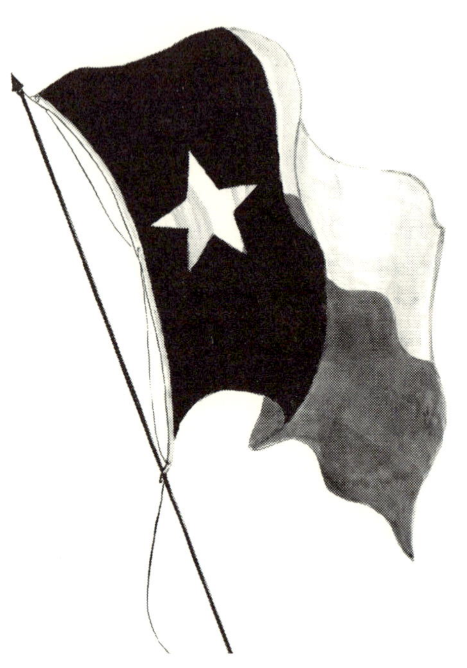

The Dark, Dark Castle

The prison camps of all the world have struck
Cold terror in the hearts of thinking men.
But for the grace of God, we might well say,
So might the prison that some soldier knew
Have been the prison for our own free lives.
What things have stood between us and the filth
Of prison beds and foul latrines of war?
What element of time has blessed our lives?
What answer, what intelligence, what plan
Has made the difference? We do not know.
We cannot understand the scope of life
Or the despair of death, or all creation —
Or even faith, if we profess a faith.
But we have always felt a sure revulsion
Of the living death the prisons hold —
The dark, dark castle and the barbed wire fence,
Wherever they may be, bring awe and fear,
For nothing is so loathsome as the foe
Who tortures crippled, sick humanity
Or holds it fast within his prison walls to rot.

Yet, in direct relation to our fears
Is knowledge that there can be decency
In camps where prisoners of war are kept.
The international code of Christian lands
Has argued for protection of the weak
And has laid out and put to action plans
To curb the suffering of men in camps.

Despite — and yet related to our fears,
Is that great admiration which we feel
For men who have survived the living hell
Of prison camps. And even greater still,
Is that emotion which is manifest

In all free men — that catch, that sudden thrill
For one who frees himself from castle walls,
For one who can escape his tormentors
And live to tell his story: hours of prayer
And courage, days of making hidden plans,
Sacrifices over and above
Those which seem possible in man, —
The risk, the plunge, the long suspense, and then
The sunlight and the clean and pleasant air
That touch his tearstreaked, joyous face again!

Back in the year of 1843,
Life was the symbol, so the order read,
Of white beans drawn by Colonel Fisher's men.
One hundred and fifty-nine were given life —
Were given life to live as prisoners
As they took up, again, their arduous march
To Mexico City. Texans, tied in pairs,
Were strongly guarded. Far too weak to march
As they were forced to march, they sometimes fell.
Then bayonets were used to get them up.
Again they slept, or tried to sleep at night
In rooms or pens so crude and vermin-filled
That further life seemed undesirable,
Except for their belief that once they reached
The courts of Mexico they would be freed.
Perhaps some officers had said as much,
Perhaps they only lived in hopes and dreams.

At last they reached the city, where they felt
Relieved and joyful that the march was done.
They had some little money which the guards
Permitted them to spend for extra food.
They bought ice cream and cakes, and long
They talked the wonders of such things
As cake and cream and memories of home.

But days passed by, the guards grew strange and cold.
Some days they had no food. At night they slept

On dirty blankets on the open walks
Or pavement of the streets. Mosquitoes struck
In swarms. There was no rest and no release.
One day a company of cavalry
Arrived. A large, sealed packet was proferred
The captain of the guard. The prisoners
Immediately were told to march. They took
Their dirty blankets and their sheepskin rolls
And journeyed down the street, a file of lancers,
Mounted and alert, on either side
Of them. The order had been sent for them
To go, as prisoners of war, for miles
To a strong castle of Perote. Santa Anna
Ordered such a thing. There was no way
Of turning back. There was a march ahead,
A march of some one hundred and sixty miles
Of hell.

In time the prisoners were told
That they might hire donkeys, which they rode
Without a bridle or a saddle. Weary
And distraught, they traveled through the mountains.
Ironically, they passed the very spot
Where General Mexia's body lay. His grave
Was pointed out to them. They thought
Of how he had so kindly tended them
When they were lost. Although Mexia then
Had captured them, he had revolted since
Against the cruelty of Santa Anna.

He had even made two tries to raise
A force with which to overthrow the man
Who was the cruel master of the land . . .
Mexia, when captured, had been taken out
And shot, for staunchly he had last refused
To quit the fight against the General.
A grand old soldier then, Mexia had said
"I will oppose you and your ways as long
As I have an arm to strike for liberty."

Their friend was dead, and they were prisoners,
Bound for the dark, dark Castle of Perote.
This castle, which had stood one hundred years,
Was very strong. Its walls were sixty feet in height
And eight feet thick, of stone so very hard
That toughest steel could scarcely make a dent
In it. A moat below the castle walls
Went down for twenty feet, and it was wide —
It measured a full two hundred feet across.
The only means of crossing such a moat
Was by the drawbridge, which was operated
From the castle side. Another wall
Of stone encircled all this yawning hole.
Some fifty feet beyond the wall of stone,
A wooden palisade of cedar timbers
Twelve feet long stood upright in the ground.
Beyond the palisade was one more ditch.
And all about this fierce and mighty tomb
Were eighty pieces of artillery.

At last they saw it, and their dread was great.
The drawbridge was put down for them to cross.
A blast of bugles and the roll of drums
Accompanied their approach onto the plaza.
They were marched before the castle governor.
It was here they met, in rags and heavy chains,
Some fifty other Texans taken captive
By General Woll at San Antonio.
A quick roll call of Fisher's men was made,
Then they were numbered and marched off to stay
In a dungeon cell. Just next to them,
The San Antonio men were prisoners.
Theirs was a similar and filthy cell.

Everything was solid stone — the floor,
The ceiling, and the walls. One little door
Was furnished each great cell. And there was one
Small loophole — nothing more. No ray of sunlight
Ever entered there. The air was cold.

Dazed and blinded in their gloomy cell,
The prisoners huddling close together stayed
Beside the door, almost afraid to move.

In time their eyes became adjusted well
To such a place. They moved around their cell,
Exploring walls and floor. They learned the truth
Of their impenetrable tomb of solid stone,
Then sank upon the cold, hard floor and slept
In fitful sleep. So passed their first long night
Within the dark, dark Castle of Perote.

The governor of the castle summoned them
When morning came. They were so weak and chilled
They hardly stood in line. The brightness hurt
Their eyes. Their line would seem to weave at times.
His order soon was read aloud to them.
They were to be chained in heavy irons,
Fastened two by two, — one by the right foot,
And the other by the left. They tried
To smile to cover up their hate — and some
Were able to give comrades needed hope
By jesting that their chains were jewelry.

Long hours after chains were riveted,
The Texans sat and planned a way to get
Them off. At length, the blacksmith could be bribed,
And leaden rivets replaced those of iron.
They rubbed and blackened leaden ones with charcoal,
Which looked like iron, but they could be removed.
Some men broke their chains by pounding them
Upon a stone with a lost cannon ball
Which they had found within their darkened cell.

Once freed from chains, they put them well aside
Except when visitors were thought to be
Approaching. They learned the usual, expected time
For officers to come. Each man learned speed
At jumping for his "jewelry." The warden

Threatened them about the punishment
Which would be theirs if chains were cast aside,
But they continued in their way of life
Such freedom as they could afford themselves, —
For they were born to freedom, and its use
Was ever to be close upon their hearts.

Some days elapsed, and then the men were told
That they would have to work. Their first impulse
Was to rebel before they would be slaves
To Mexicans. However, they were soon
At work. They used wheelbarrows and took filth
Outside the castle. After this was done,
Like horses, they were harnessed to haul rocks.
Each wagon had a team of twenty-five,
And they were made to go up mountainsides
To get the rocks the Mexicans desired
For fortifications which they wished repaired.

Despite their labor and imprisonment,
The men would not forget to have their fun.
McFall, a large and energetic man,
Was "lead horse" of one team of twenty-five.
He was forever "getting scared," and he
Would "run away" and bang the wagon around
In such a way to knock the corners off
Adobe houses. Even officers
Of the Mexicans would laugh when men
Who owned the houses would rush out and scream
Their curses in bad Spanish.

                      At other times
A team would stop dead still and shed its reins
And harness in the middle of a street.
Half of the men would hurry to the right
For drinks; the other half would journey left.
When they were driven out of one saloon,
They simply traded sides across the street.
The overseers could not keep them up
Or keep up with them. So they laughed and sighed!

Most overseers were downcast convicts
Who seemed to sympathize and to enjoy
The Texan brand of fun. They had so little
Pleasure for themselves. Each convict had
A frightening lash, but it was seldom used.
There were two reasons — one already named.
The other was the convict's fear to hit
A Texan. Some several times a Texan, lashed,
Had jumped his overseer and beat him up.
The convicts did not often strike the men!

The work the Texans did was not too hard,
But they resented working for their foe.
They usually complied to get fresh air
And sunlight, but occasionally some man
Would sooner die than work. Dan Henrie said
That he had never put stones on the mountains
And "he'd be shot if he took any away."
He scratched his legs with a steel writing pen
Which he had found upon an officer's desk.
The scratches, knee to ankle, were inflamed
After wrappings of old shirts and blankets
Had infected them. The morning after
When the order came for him to work,
He was hardly able to stand up. His legs
Were swollen and quite sore. His work that day
Was, as a consequence, his very last.

Some troubles with the Texans kept them in
From time to time, and there were rainy days
When outdoor work was hardly possible.
With more confinement, men were less at ease.
Their health declined enough that finally
A virulent fever spread throughout the cells.
Eighteen men died of it, and they were buried
In the ditch beside the castle wall.
Only three escaped the dread disease.

One prisoner told the horrors of the fever.

He was unconscious for some fourteen days
Of the thirty he was ill. He prayed for death
As he was left upon a hard couch far from home,
Unattended and uncared for — sick.

With added trouble, cruel treatment came.
The food was scarce and hardly edible, —
The meat so rotten it would stick like glue
When thrown against a wall. With all of this,
The men planned ways to keep their spirits up.
They sang and danced for hours every day
To the music of a violin,
Accompanied by their clanking prison chains.
'Rosin the Bow,' a favorite song of theirs,
Was sung so loud the officers complained.

A diary, or a journal, one man kept
Set down the routine of their weary days.
At one time he explained their changing rooms
So officers could check for holes in walls
Or floors. This was in 1844,
The first of August. On the second day
Of August, he reported carpenters
At work outside the castle. They were chained
By two and two. Upon the third, no food
Was given to the men. Then, by the sixth,
They had to move again. Nine men were sent
Into the mountains to get brooms one day.
They wanted to escape, but there was not
A chance for it. The fifteenth was mail day
But no mail came for them. (It sometimes did.
They *had* heard news from home.)

                The sixteenth day
Was quite prosaic as he wrote "wash day";
But then he added more, "I have learned
Today that the men in room No. 7 are trying
To dig their way out. (I am in No. 8.)"

Upon the nineteenth day he wrote with spirit

Of a willingness to risk his life
In order to accomplish freedom.

                                    Soon,
There was more trouble. On the twenty-third,
When fifteen men went off for mountain rock,
Two men ran off. "Thurmond was run down,"
He wrote, "and brought back in about two hours.
We have not yet heard any word of Bush.
The major of this post now says that we
Shall not receive more money from our friends,
Nor cook more food again in our own way."

And so the long, long days dragged on and on
Until the government of Mexico
Released the Texans one September day
On the anniversary of their victory
For national independence won from Spain.

Of all the men at Mier who drew white beans,
There were just thirty-five left to be freed.
It was the fall of 1844
Before the Texans made their homeward trek.

One story has been told of their release
Which indicates that there was sympathy
For them, — so greatly felt, so long expressed
By Santa Anna's beautiful young wife
That her request was granted as she lay
Upon her deathbed. Santa Anna cleared
The Texan prisoners from the castle cells —
Yet, on and on, the shadows of Perote
Indirectly touched his life with grief.

But there were some with daring General Green
Who had escaped more than a year before
The others were released. The thrilling tale
Of their courageous and miraculous
Escape, made on the night of July second,
In 1843, is one of the strangest

Of all records made by fugitives.
Perhaps their cunning methods brought a watch
Far closer on the ones who stayed behind.
A soldier's journal mentioned changing rooms
As a requirement for the periodic checks
Of guards and officers. At any rate,
There were sixteen who made good their escape,
And eight of those sixteen with General Green
Were able to get back to Texas homes.

What labor was involved in that escape!
The men took time about at chipping stone;
One man at a time, by lying prone
And resting on his elbows, could perform
The arduous task of boring, breaking chips.
These were so small that the yield of one day's work
Could never measure quite a hatful. The chips
Each workman broke away were kept by him
And buried under loose brick in the floor.
A strict routine of continuous work was kept,
And each man knew the time his turn would come.
Carpenter's chisels, their only tools, were poor
In quality. They had been smuggled in
Under blankets of the prisoners,
But progress, although painful, came to be
Enough to keep the men upon the job.
A laborer would often work while strained
Until his nerveless hand would drop the tool,
His elbow would give way, and he would sob
With weakness, his face against the very thick
And unrelenting stone.

                                Finally,
A hollow sound, like music in their ears,
Denoted that the end was drawing close.
Now they worked to keep from breaking through
The thin and shell-like section which was left.

And all this time, supplies had been concealed.
Sugar, bacon, and chocolate had been bought

With money sent by a friend in Mexico.
The prison bread was saved and stored away,
As every effort was kept up to make
Their stores enough for a two weeks' supply.

A heavy walking cane of sapote wood
For every man had been made possible
By carpenters who worked odd times at them
And secreted them against the fateful night
When they should be required. They were the weapons
Of defense, along with pocket knives—
The only two things which a man could have
For self-protection from the enemy.

According to their plan, the men should go
In squads of two or three, once they were out.
This separation would make their escape
More easily attainable, and quick
Detection by the soldiers much less likely.
The flight began the night of July second
After some uncertainty. Several
Of the men who planned to go when plans
Were first set up, now wavered, thinking back
Upon the consequences other men
Had known for such an act. Sixteen resolved
To go, whatever should become of them.

"At half-past five o'clock," says General Green,
"I took leave of my friends." (Green's records left
About the dangerous escape is stranger
Than the wild imaginings of men
Whose timeless fiction and whose ageless art
Have thrilled mankind for generations past.)
The prisoners were sad in their goodbyes.
The ones who were to stay could not believe
That General Green would make good his escape.
They tried to show their confidence, but some
Broke down and big hearts overflowed. All men,
Those going and those to remain, were mute

In last farewells. Their rugged, workworn hands
Were grasped, and all were prayerful for the flight.

At six o'clock the jailer came to see
That all the prisoners were there. The count
Was made as usual, and everything
Was found secure. He spoke a quick "bueno,"
And tension eased at once among the men.

But what a night it was! A chilling rain
Fell fast with darkness, — but the rain to them
Was good, for it caused castle guards to seek
The light and warmth of indoors. It was right
That they should go at such a time. Perhaps
It was an act of God. At seven o'clock
The flight began. The thin shell of the wall
Was broken through, the prisoners attached a rope
By which they could go down into the moat.
But there was yet delay — two hours more —
To widen the outside opening of the wall,
For only those who were the smallest men
Could get their bodies through the outside breach.

"John Toowig got into the breach," wrote Green.
"Feet foremost, and, drawing his bundle after him,
Inch by inch he squeezed and let himself down
Hand over hand about thirty feet to the bottom
Of the moat." The others followed Toowig
But all were forced to be incredibly slow
Because of the depth and smallness of the hole.
The act was fraught with possible defeat
When twice disaster threatened. Isaac Allen
Almost fell upon the men below.
"Stand from under, boys, I cannot say
Whether these hands are going to hold," he called,
And soon he fell. But sand down in the moat
Was ankle-deep. His fall was broken well
And he got up unhurt. A fortunate man,
He had been able to conceal a gun

And get it down with him, but the extra weight
And the care in handling it required of him
Were weakening.

                              The case of Samuel Stone,
More serious by far, caused great concern.
He was determined to make his escape,
But he was large and could not make his way
Unaided through the breach. He was stuck fast,
Unable to get backward or to go
Ahead. The prisoners inside the room
Who were assisting men in their escape
Tied ropes around his hands and drew him back.
But he would not be left. He told the men
About his wife and children. He convinced them
That he would sooner die than lose this chance.
"I will go through," he said — and shed his clothes.
"I'll go or leave no skin upon my bones."
He made a second effort and got through,
Leaving his torn flesh around the breach.
By half-past twelve o'clock all men were down.
They crossed the yawning moat and outer wall
And finally were upon the open land.
The record tells of cheers and muffled cries
Which had to be suppressed, — of how at last
They gave vent to their feelings, jumping up
And clicking heels, time and again, for joy.

Through friends, arrangements had been made for a guide
And horses to get them on to Vera Cruz,
But they were disappointed. They split up
In pairs, said their farewells, and parted there.
Some were never to get through or meet
The others once again on Texas soil. Some
Were recaptured soon and taken back
Where punishment was very hard for them.

The rest of Green's account deals principally
With several of the Texans who escaped.

Daniel Henrie, who started out with Green,
Was one of these. The other two were met
Some eight miles later. They were John Toowig
And Charles K. Reese. The four went to the mountains,
For the risk elsewhere was very great.

Thin goatskin slippers, the only kind afforded
Castle prisoners, were good enough
When worn inside, but soon they fell apart
As the men continued walking through wet grass
And over stones. He wrote of their suffering much
From mountain climbing, for sore feet and long
Imprisonment combined to weaken them
In mountain air, but they kept on. He wrote:
"Before it was fairly light we had reached a point
Some distance above the settlements; and our tracks
Having been effaced by rain, we felt reasonably
Secure; and selecting a dark cove, lay down to rest.

"It was near sundown when we resumed our journey,
Thinking it more safe to travel by night than by day.
But we escaped one danger only to fall
Into another . . . Inaccessible mountains
And bottomless ravines followed hard
Upon each other, and at times stopped further progress.

"We usually traveled single file, each in turn
Taking the lead," he said. "One dark night
When it was my turn to lead, we fell
Into a level path, which we pursued
Several hundred yards. We could not see
The length of our arms ahead of us, so I
Kept the end of my walking stick always
About two feet ahead of me, feeling the way.
At length I felt no bottom. I stopped as quick
As thought, and drawing back a step, called
To my companions to halt. Then, stooping down,
With my stick I reached as far as my arm allowed
But still found no bottom. Lying flat

On our faces and straining our eyes,
We discovered what we took to be
The tops of trees far below. This discovery
Gave us a great fright. We were on the brink
Of one of those frightful precipices, and a single
False step might plunge us headlong into the depths.
We now changed our course and felt our way,
Inch by inch, down a steep descent
Of at least a mile into a valley
Which lay at the base of the precipice.

"Even as I write, the remembrance of that dreadful
Situation unnerves me. One step more
And myself, then Reese, and then Dan would have fallen
A thousand feet — for no alarm from the foremost
Would have reached the next — leaving no one on earth
A knowledge of our destiny.

                    "Daylight
Found us lying under our wet blankets
In some thick bushes. Here we rested a few hours,
Being much exhausted and suffering greatly for want
Of refreshment. In our descent from the mountain
We frequently slipped and fell with great violence;
And our feet and legs were skinned, swollen, and sore.
From a small creek running near by our hiding place
We got water and, lighting a fire, made cup
After cup of coffee, which greatly relieved us.
We then bathed our bruises and had a good chat,
The first since we left the castle, which restored
Our spirits and strengthened our courage to proceed
On our journey."

                    General Green believed
That they were near the city of Jalapa,
"And we had not gone many miles," he wrote,
"From our cooking place when our conjecture was
Found to be correct. We heard the ringing
Of the city bells, of which there are great numbers
In every Mexican town, and by the bright moonlight

Saw the city itself spread out before us,
Resting peacefully in the lap of the mountains.

"It was our plan to leave the city to the right,
Strike into the river valley, which our map
Showed led to the seacoast, and thence follow
It down.

       "We bore to the left to avoid the city,
But soon found ourselves in a maze of stone fences
Covered with briers and prickly pear by which
Our feet were cruelly lacerated. The farther
We proceeded, the thicker, it appeared
To us, became the settlements; so we
Resolved to play our game boldly and strike
For the heart of the city.

         "Indian file,
We passed up one street and down another,
Our broad-brim sombreros pulled down over our eyes
And our shoulders and knapsacks covered with blankets,
After the fashion of the Mexicans.
To the frequent challenge of the sentinels
We made no reply, but kept our course
In silence."

      It appeared to General Green
That there were more dogs in Jalapa
Than he had ever seen in other towns.
The dogs barked angrily and ran at them
As if to point them out as foreigners,
But fortunately the canes of sapote wood
Kept the barking dogs a distance back.

Green's record then continues with details
Of how they found a hiding place at last
After wandering about the city
Until near daylight. They found a hill,
A little round-top hill with weeds and brush,
South of the town. It looked deserted there,
So they lay down in rain-drenched weeds to sleep.

They were so tired they had no other choice
Than to lie down in cold and soaking clothes
With their wet blankets. They rested all that day.
At dusk they wandered back into the town.

He tells of how they went to an old church
Which had high weeds around two sides. There he
And Reese stayed well obscured and very quiet.
There was a friend — if they could find that friend —
Who would receive and care for them. Dan found
His house and brought the friend to talk to Green,
Who wrote of him with caution as Don —.
"The Don was expecting us and took us home,"
He wrote, "where we found his good wife
Preparing us a warm supper.

                    "We remained
With these good people five days and were treated
With a kindness we shall never forget.
They gave us the best of food and all kinds
Of delicious fruits. Our feet and legs were bathed
And poulticed; and we sent out and bought good shoes
And other things necessary to our journey.
By the sixth night, we were as far recovered
From our mountain fatigues as to be able to proceed.

"At ten o'clock on this night the Don said to us,
'Prepare to follow me and ask no questions.'
We did so, and he led us through the city
Into a dark valley about two miles off,
And telling us to hide in the bushes here
He went farther on down the hollow.
When about a hundred yards away
He gave a shrill whistle, which was answered then,
And we saw — the moon shone bright — a tall, active
Well-made man spring from the rocks and join him;
After exchanging a few words, they came
In the direction of our hiding place,
And called us to come forth. 'This man,'
Said the Don, 'will conduct you to Vera Cruz.

Follow him but ask no questions. You need
Have no fear of his betraying you,
As he is one of the most noted robbers
In Mexico and he dare not show himself
To the authorities.' So saying, and wishing
Us Godspeed, the generous Don returned
To the city and we followed our mysterious guide
Down the hollow.

       "We had gone but a short distance
When, in a dismal looking place in a cross hollow,
We came upon a confederate of our guide
Holding mules, which were to be our conveyance
To the seacoast. Without speaking, the head man
Placed a bridle in our hands; we mounted
And followed on a narrow, winding path
Leading through deep ravines and broken cliffs
Until daylight, not one word passing between us
On this long ride.

       "Our robber guides now left us,
Leading away the mules and promising
To return at night to resume the journey.
We hid ourselves in a thicket, as usual,
And, after eating of the provisions
Left by our guides, lay down on the ground
And slept soundly till near night.

       "Our guides
Returned at the appointed time. At a sign
From them we mounted our mules and followed
In silence, as we had done the night before.
Nearly the whole of this night we rode
In a heavy rain, and part of the time
In a tremendous storm. Our path was narrow,
Rugged, and, at places, quite precipitous;
And so winding that in the darkness we appeared
To be merely zigzagging about, without
Making any progress. We gave our mules
Free rein and they, as if conscious

Of their responsibility, picked their way
Over ground that would have been impassable
To any other animal."

                        Five days
Passed, in which near tragedy occurred
For Green and his companions and their guides.
A great sandstorm blew up and there were times
The sand so stifled them that they were close
To death, and then it piled against their bodies
In great drifts and almost buried them.
Perhaps it was a blessing in disguise,
For they were late in reaching Vera Cruz
And some miles out of town they narrowly
Escaped recapture. A squad of cavalry
That had been sent to intercept them
Was eluded cleverly — so well
Eluded and so cleverly, they passed
Within earshot of the squad of Mexicans
And were not apprehended. Green's men hid
And their robber guides conducted them at night
To the house of a friend within the city.
They were to stay in hiding, as arranged,
Until a vessel should be in, by which
They could get passage to the United States.

Their friend in Vera Cruz was very kind —
As kind as the Don in Jalapa had been —
And they were put at ease and comforted,
But no boat was there, and days passed by.
They were like prisoners still, and yet they knew
That there was nothing to be done except
To wait. They were obliged to stay confined
In one small room despite the sweltering heat.
They dared not go outside and risk recapture,
So they stayed within their darkened room.
It had one little window and the sounds
About the city drifted in. They learned
That dreaded yellow fever was epidemic

In their quarter of the town. The bells
Tolled dismally from morn till night for those
Who died of fever and for those near death.
The rattle of the death-cart could be heard
Beneath that window, hour after hour,
Until they fancied in their stifling room
That they were victims of the dread disease.

For thirteen days of cramped and burning life
They hid in almost deathly silence there.
And then one night a knock upon their door —
Their host was with them, and with news at last.
A vessel from the United States, in port,
Would sail for New Orleans. They were to leave
That very night. Arrangements with the captain
Had been made, so they would have a place
In which to hide. The boat would sail some time
The following day. At nine o'clock that night
A detail sent to fetch them to their vessel
Took them safely to the landing, slipping them
Into a little boat which was to go
To the American ship. They were challenged
By three Mexican men-of-war close by,
But, at the risk of being fired upon,
They did not answer. Fortunately they soon
Ran alongside the American ship,
And, clambering aboard, they met a friend.
Captain Lloyd, the commander, greeted them.
He had known General Green quite well for years.
Then, happily, they found three other men
On board who had escaped the castle walls
With them — Cornegay, Forrester,
And Barclay. What a feeling of real joy
And unbelievable surprise — and humor,
Too, for Cornegay and Forrester
Had shipped as firemen and were standing there
With smutty faces and red flannel shirts,
As though they had been brought up to such jobs.

The men slept well that night, with minds at ease
But there was danger yet. When morning came
The captain told Green he would go ashore
To watch. When the inspecting officer should start
To come on board he would make a signal.
With the signal given, the prisoners
Should hide themselves. Green was to go below
And crawl beneath the boilers. This he did,
But half an hour's stem was going strong
Before the signal came. This was a spot
So dark and hot that he was forced to turn
From side to side to keep from burning up.
Five seconds was enough to scorch one side,
And then he turned, time and again, and thought
That being singed would be a better thing
Than to be taken back to castle walls —
He would not let them take him back alive.

When this ordeal was over and the ship
Was out at sea, there never was a sky
So clear to look upon. No other sea
Was ever so serene. Green's men, so bathed
In fire from months of long imprisonment
And rigorous ordeals as fugitives,
Cold never fill their eyes enough with it,
This wonder of a sailing ship at sea —
This symbol of a bird in peaceful flight —
This symbol of a thing called liberty.

Eight days of sailing, and at last they moored
At the wharves of New Orleans. Two days,
And then they shipped again. This time the boat
Upon the calm blue sea would seek the mouth
Of the Brazos River on the Texas coast.
An uneventful voyage, some sailors said.
For weather had been favorable to them —
An uneventful voyage? Perhaps — and yet,
It was a voyage which took gaunt soldiers home —
A chapter closed, a benediction lived.

Through the Years

So many fighting men of Texas go
In every age to win their fame in war!
The Texas Rangers and the National Guard
Are peacetime fighters for the good of man,
Their very presence lending dignity
And rightful caution to a way of life
That conquers evil and protects the weak;
And they are seasoned fighters of the best,
When, in the first emergency of war,
A great responsibility is theirs.

All down the ages, in our nation's need,
How many Texans answer to the call!
Look back — they fight to victory with Scott
And Taylor in the War with Mexico.
And even in a nation's civil strife,
They fight as God gives them the light to see
The truth: Dick Dowling wins a victory
To keep invaders back from Sabine Pass, —
Another scene, and Texans hear the words:
"My fighting Texas boys!" from one they love,
And how they fight by General Robert E. Lee!

And many another scene of war is theirs:
They fight with Teddy Roosevelt who goes
With his Rough Riders over San Juan Hill.
And now they fly in planes, they march, or sail —
They help to quell each threat to liberty
And life in all the hot spots of the world.

But greatly, dearly do they strive to bring
The flag of freedom out and keep it there —
In World War I and World War II they fight,
Whether in the thick of Belleau Woods
Or Battle of the Bulge, some years beyond.

Remember yet the men on Egypt's desert
Or far across the world in Saipan's hell —
In frozen waste of Korea's nameless war —
Or horrors of a war in Vietnam —
They have a way of being what they are,
For Fighting Men of Texas are, in truth,
A living legend in a way of life
That fights for right and freedom through the years.

Exploration (January, 1986)

Fighting men of Texas long explored
The frontiers of the land — the land they *won*;
Yet, exploration moving ever on,
Reaching high into the boundlessness of space,
Now centers for Americans in NASA's arms.
Her great space center built on Texas soil
(Along with other national points of power)
Controls the missions of the astronauts
And those who build technologies and dreams.

Yet, as we see a shuttle launch today,
A horror bursts across the wide blue sky
And we are sorely grieved that death has struck.

We later bow to mourn the seven lost,
The seven* *Challenger* so proudly housed,
As services proceed at NASA's home . . .
This home, years back, was then alive with joy,
While linked with tracking astronauts in space
Or bringing pictures of the "giant leap"
Of those who proudly walked upon the moon.

So, what of exploration in this year?
Of lives and fortunes buried in the sea?"
Our history, punctuated with defeat,
Will carry on again in NASA's wake . . .
Remember, exploration never was
An easy path — from early times to now —
Yet fallen heroes have been known to rise
As others — for them — reach to climb again!

---

* *The seven:* Dick Scobee, Michael Smith, Judith Resnik, Ellison Onizuka, Ronald McNair, Gregory Jarvis, and Christa McAuliffe.

Envoy

O Sons of Fighting Men, of pioneers:
Those tragic fighters who saw no reward
Live on in you, in triumph, and in death.
They borned a spirit in the minds and hearts
Of all who made the new Republic live.

If any war be useless war; or yet,
If men should come to judge the need to fight
By principles of profit rather than
Those of humanity and Christian laws,
It might well be our loss would come. What then
Of Texans — and this long-loved native land?